Quick-n-Easy

MEXICAN

RECIPES

MARVELOUS MEXICAN MEALS—IN MINUTES!

by

Susan K. Bollin

GOLDEN WEST ☼
PUBLISHERS

Cover photo by Dick Dietrich

Cover design by The Book Studio

Artwork by Steve Parker

Other cookbooks by Susan K. Bollin:

Chip and Dip Lovers Cook Book

Salsa Lovers Cook Book

Sedona Cook Book

Library of Congress Cataloging-in-Publication Data
Bollin, Susan K.
Quick-n-Easy Mexican Recipes: Marvelous Mexican meals, in just minutes! / by Susan K. Bollin.
    p.   cm.
Includes index.
ISBN 0-914846-85-X: $6.95
1. Cookery, Mexican. 2. Quick and Easy Cookery.   I. Title.
TX716.M4B594   1993   93-21427
641.5972 —dc20   CIP

Printed in the United States of America

ISBN 13: 978-0-914846-85-7
ISBN 10: 0-914846-85-X

27th Printing © 2008

Golden West Publishers, Inc.
4113 N. Longview Ave.
Phoenix, AZ 85014, USA
(602) 265-4392
(800)658-5830

For free sample recipes for every Golden West cookbook, visit our website:
www.goldenwestpublishers.com

Introduction

People have fallen in love with Mexican food. Even the name stirs the imagination with warm and colorful images.

Mexico is an exciting and vibrant country, known for its music, art, beautiful beaches and, especially, its marvelous foods. It is not surprising that Mexican food is the most popular and most widely accepted of all ethnic foods. With Mexican food products now widely available, these dishes are easy to prepare and are within the reach of all food budgets.

Today's busy lifestyles do not allow most people the luxury of time needed to make tortillas, roast chiles and grind corn. Even so, it isn't necessary to sacrifice the pleasure of preparing and enjoying Mexican foods at home.

This is a collection of quick and easy Mexican recipes for today's busy families. With practice, many of the recipes can be adapted to suit individual tastes, such as using more or less chiles, the substitution of beef for chicken and choices of seasonings. Many of the ingredients used in these recipes can be kept on a shelf or in a freezer. Stocking up is a good idea. When the Mexican food craving hits it will be nice to know the ingredients for quick Mexican food meals are at hand!

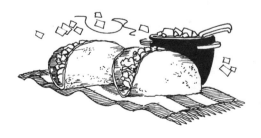

Contents

Breakfasts

Appetizers, Spreads & Marinades

Soups & Salads

Breads

Main Dishes

Side Dishes

Desserts

Beverages

Glossary

A glossary of common Mexican foods, seasonings and ingredients

ALLSPICE: Allspice got its name because its fragrance and flavor resemble a combination of several other spices. Its most common use is in pastries and sweet salsa.

BASIL: Basil is a versatile herb with a sweet minty flavor that is especially good combined with tomatoes.

BUÑUELOS: Similar to a fritter and frequently used as a dessert.

BURRO, BURRITO: Flour tortillas filled with a mixture of choice, folded and rolled and frequently topped with a variety of salsas and vegetables.

BEANS *(FRIJOLES)*: Along with corn, beans are one of the most important ingredients of Mexican cooking. Here are some of the most common varieties.

> **Anasazi:** One of the oldest Indian beans, dark red and white in color.

> **Black:** Also called turtle beans, they are a very dark purple.

> **Pinto:** The best known and most common, they are native to the southwestern United States. Pinto means painted and these beans are mottled pink and brown in color.

> **White:** These common beans are also known as Navy beans and are used all over the country.

BEANS, REFRIED *(FRIJOLES REFRITOS)*: The most commonly served beans in restaurants. Cooked beans that have been cooked a second time by frying.

CAFÉ: Coffee

CALABAZA: A vegetable known as Mexican squash or pumpkin and interchangeable with Zucchini in recipes.

CARNE: Meat

CARNITAS: "Little Meats"—cooked pork that has been roasted and shredded.

CERVEZA: Beer

CEVICHE: Raw, chilled and marinated fish or seafood.

CHAYOTE: A pear-shaped, light green squash interchangeable with scalloped-edge (Patty-Pan) squash.

CHEESE: *Queso*

CHILE: The most characteristic ingredient of Mexican foods, technically the "fruit" of the chile plant but commonly referred to as a vegetable. There are hundreds of varieties worldwide.

CHILI: A combination of spices, as in Chili Powder or a descriptive cooking term, as in Chili con Carne.

CHILE CON QUESO: Chiles mixed with cheese, frequently served as an appetizer.

CHILE RELLENO: A chile filled with a stuffing and cooked.

CHIMICHANGA: A tortilla, usually flour, filled with a mixture of choice, folded and deep fried or baked until crispy.

CHORIZO: A spicy Mexican sausage.

CILANTRO (CORIANDER): Cilantro is the leaf of the Coriander plant. Coriander seeds have a very different flavor than that of cilantro. These are ancient herbs that are also known as Chinese Parsley. They are among the most widely used spices in the world and one of the ingredients of curry powder. The dried form, whether powder or seeds, should be stored in the refrigerator.

CINNAMON: Cinnamon is used in both powdered and whole, or stick, form. A must for Mexican chocolate, it is one of the most popular of the spices. It is widely used in desserts and other sweets. The ground form should be stored in the refrigerator.

CLOVES: Cloves add a wonderful sweet and spicy taste to many Mexican foods. Used either whole or powdered, cloves are one of the world's most popular spices.

CORN: *Maíz*

CUCUMBER: *Pepino*

CUMIN: Comino. Cumin is native to the Mediterranean, as are many other spices and herbs used with chiles. It has been cultivated for thousands of years. In addition to its wide use in

Mexican foods, it is also common in Spanish and Chinese cooking. Cumin should be stored in the refrigerator.

EMPANADA: A turnover, usually filled with a meat, vegetable or sweet filling.

ENCHILADA: A tortilla, usually corn, filled with any combination and rolled or stacked in layers.

ENCHILADA, FLAT: A thick, pancake-like masa mixture, formed into a patty, deep fried and served with Salsa roja.

ENSALADA: A salad.

FLAN: A caramel custard dessert.

FLAUTA: Corn tortillas filled with a mixture, usually a meat mixture, rolled up to resemble a flute and fried until crisp.

FRIJOLE: Bean. *Frijole negro* is a black bean; *frijole blanco* is a white bean.

FRITO: Fried

GUACAMOLE: An avocado mixture frequently served as an appetizer with chips or as a garnish.

HELADO: Ice cream

HUEVO: Egg

JALAPEÑO: A very popular medium sized hot chile.

JICAMA: An apple-like, mild tasting vegetable that is frequently used in salads.

LECHE: Milk

MANGO: A popular tropical fruit.

MAÍZ: Corn

MASA: Corn flour that has been treated. It is used to make tortillas, flat enchiladas and tamales.

NACHOS: Tortilla chips topped with various mixtures and usually served as an appetizer.

OREGANO: Oregano is an herb made from the dried leaves of a variety of the Marjoram family. It is used in Mexican and in Mediterranean cuisine and is especially good with tomatoes, cheese, eggs and pork. It should be stored in the refrigerator.

PAPAYA: A popular tropical fruit.

PINE NUTS: *Piñons.* A nut crop native to southwestern United States.

PINEAPPLE: *Piña*

POLLO: Chicken

QUESADILLA: A tortilla, with a filling, folded in half and fried or grilled.

QUESO: Cheese

RICE: *Arroz*

SALSA: A Mexican sauce, the kinds and uses of which are unlimited.

SOPAIPILLA: A deep fried, puffy bread, frequently served as a dessert with honey or other sweet dessert salsa.

TACO: A tortilla, usually corn, that is folded in half, fried and then filled.

TAMALE: Masa filled with a choice of filling, wrapped in corn husks and steamed until cooked.

TOMATILLO: A small, firm green tomato-like fruit which is covered with a papery husk. Along with the tomato, the tomatillo is the most popular ingredient in salsas.

TORTILLA: A thin pancake-like bread, either corn or flour, that is the basis of most southwestern and Mexican dishes.

TOSTADA: A fried tortilla served flat and topped with a variety of mixtures.

TOPOPO: A fried tortilla, usually corn, topped with salad ingredients - a Mexican salad.

Breakfasts

Huevos Rancheros

Everyone has their own ideas about how to make these delicious eggs and when to eat them. They make a great waker-upper breakfast, a wonderful lunch or a light supper.

2 Tbsp. VEGETABLE OIL
2 corn TORTILLAS, fried
4 EGGS
1/2 cup LONGHORN or JACK CHEESE, grated
SALSA

In a medium skillet, fry tortillas in hot oil. Drain on paper towels. Fry eggs, 2 at a time, in the same skillet. When cooked to desired degree of doneness, place 2 eggs on each tortilla. Top with grated cheese. Serve with salsa.

Serves 2.

Breakfast in Mexico is called DESAYUNO, lunch is called ALMUERZO, dinner is known as COMIDA and supper is CENA.

Mexican Breakfast Eggs

4 Tbsp. BUTTER or MARGARINE
8 EGGS
3 Tbsp. MILK
4 Tbsp. SALSA
1 cup crushed TORTILLA CHIPS

Melt butter in a large skillet over medium heat. In a bowl, beat eggs, add milk and salsa. Pour into skillet and stir occasionally until eggs are thoroughly cooked. Stir in chips.

Serves 4.

Daybreak Burritos

4 flour TORTILLAS, 10-12 inch size
1/2 lb. CHORIZO
3 EGGS
2 Tbsp. MILK
1 JALAPEÑO, peeled, seeded and diced
1/2 cup sharp CHEDDAR CHEESE, grated

Place tortillas on 4 plates. In a medium skillet, fry chorizo until thoroughly cooked. Drain any excess fat. In a bowl, beat eggs with milk, add jalapeño and pour into skillet. Scramble egg mixture with chorizo until eggs are cooked. Place equal amounts on each tortilla, top with cheese. Roll, tube style, and eat like a sandwich.

Serves 4.

Chorizo is a spicy Mexican sausage usually made from pork, but may be made from both pork and beef.

Breakfast Burritos

6 sm. flour TORTILLAS, about 7" in diameter
12 EGGS
1 can (7 oz.) diced GREEN CHILES, drained
2 TOMATOES, chopped
1 cup JACK CHEESE, grated
SALT and PEPPER
SALSA

Warm tortillas, set aside. Scramble eggs and chiles together. When eggs are cooked, divide them equally onto each tortilla. Place tomatoes and cheese, divided equally, over the egg mixture. Salt and pepper to taste. Roll each tortilla. Serve with salsa.

Serves 6.

Green Chile Omelet

4 EGGS, beaten
4 Tbsp. MILK
1 can (4 oz.) diced GREEN CHILES or 1 sm. JALAPEÑO,
    seeded and diced

Beat eggs and milk, pour into non-stick, pre-heated pan. When ready to fold, place chiles on omelet. Fold and cook until done. Serve with salsa.

Serves 2.

Salsa means sauce in Spanish and is one of the most popular of all Mexican dishes. There are endless kinds of salsas, many of which are easy to make at home.

Breakfast Rolls

6 flour TORTILLAS, any size
ORANGE JUICE
CINNAMON SUGAR

Brush one side of each tortilla with orange juice. Sprinkle with cinnamon sugar. Roll and microwave on high for 30 seconds.

Serves 2-6.

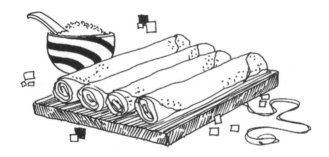

Fritole

SOURDOUGH ROLLS, allow 2 rolls per serving,
**   depending upon the size of the rolls**
1 can (15 oz.) REFRIED BEANS (frijoles) with or without
**   jalapeños, according to taste**
2 cups JACK CHEESE, grated
sliced, pickled JALAPEÑOS

Cut rolls in half, spread frijoles on rolls. Cover with grated cheese, dot top with jalapeños. Broil until cheese melts.

Breakfast Burritos with Sausage & Potatoes

(Chorizo y Papas)

4 (10-12 inch) FLOUR TORTILLAS
1/2 lb. MEXICAN SAUSAGE (CHORIZO)
1/4 cup ONION, diced
2 med. RED POTATOES (PAPAS), diced
4 lg. EGGS
1/4 cup MILK

Place tortillas on four dinner plates. In medium skillet, crumble chorizo and fry until cooked. Drain well in colander. Add onions and potatoes to skillet; cover and cook over medium heat until potatoes are tender and onions are limp and slightly browned. In a small bowl, beat eggs with milk. Add to potatoes and onions and scramble until eggs are cooked. Add sausage to potato mixture and heat, stirring well. Place equal amounts of mixture in each tortilla. Roll tortillas and serve at once.

Serves 4.

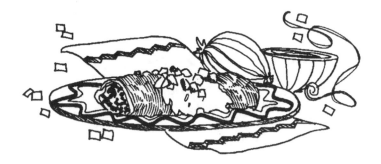

Appetizers,
Spreads
&
Marinades

Homemade Chips

Traditional Method

Cut corn tortillas into quarters and fry in vegetable oil until crispy. Drain on paper towels and salt to taste.

Ranch Method

Dip whole corn tortillas in water. While dripping, cut into quarters. Arrange on cookie sheet, single layered, and bake in preheated 450 degree oven for approximately 6 minutes, turning after 3 minutes or until crispy. Salt if desired.

Instant Flour Tortillas

1 pkg. REFRIGERATOR BISCUITS, any kind
FLOUR

Roll out biscuits on lightly floured surface until very thin. Grill in heated frying pan until lightly browned on each side.

Patio Dip

1 pt. dry COTTAGE CHEESE (not creamed)
1 can (4 oz.) diced GREEN CHILES or 1 sm. JALAPEÑO,
    seeded and diced
1/2 cup MAYONNAISE
3 GREEN ONIONS, diced
1 med. TOMATO, diced
2 Tbsp. prepared SALSA

Combine all ingredients. Serve chilled with tortilla chips.

Makes 2 1/2 cups.

Chile con Queso I

2 Tbsp. OLIVE OIL
1 med. ONION, diced
1 can (7 oz.) diced GREEN CHILES
1 cup LONGHORN CHEESE, grated (1 cup = 1/2 lb.)
1 cup canned TOMATOES, drained and chopped
1/2 cup heavy CREAM

Sauté onions in olive oil in a medium size skillet until limp but not brown. Turn heat to Low, add chiles, cheese, tomatoes and cream. Stir until cheese is melted. Pour into a fondue pot and serve with chips.

Makes about 2 cups.

Note: Chile con Queso is also delicious served over vegetables and baked fish.

Chile con Queso II

1/2 cup OLIVE OIL
1/2 cup ONIONS, chopped
1 GARLIC CLOVE, crushed
1 JALAPEÑO, seeded and diced or
1 can (7 oz.) diced GREEN CHILES, drained
1 sm. can TOMATO PASTE
1 can (28 oz.) TOMATOES, drained
1 can (15 oz.) TOMATOES AND GREEN CHILES, drained
1/2 lb. LONGHORN CHEESE

Sauté onions and garlic in olive oil until lightly browned. Add remaining ingredients, except cheese, and simmer until medium thick. Cut cheese in pieces, add to mixture and simmer until ropey. This dip should be kept warm in mini-crockpot or fondue pot.

Makes 4 cups.

Chile con Queso III

8 oz. PROCESSED CHEESE, cubed
1 can (4 oz.) diced GREEN CHILES
ONION SALT

Place cubed cheese in microwaveable bowl. Melt cheese, stir in chiles. Add onion salt to taste.

Makes about 2 cups.

Note: This dip should be kept warm while serving.

Chile con Queso IV

This makes a quick and easy festive fondue.

1 pkg. (1 lb.) Mexican style VELVEETA®
1 jar (4 oz.) PIMENTOS, diced
6 GREEN ONIONS, diced

Melt Velveeta in fondue pot. Stir in pimentos and onions. Serve with chips.

Quick Dip

1 pt. SOUR CREAM
2 cans MEXICAN BEAN DIP

Combine and stir well. Serve with chips or use as a topping for tostadas.

Makes 3 cups.

Quesadillas

FLOUR TORTILLAS, any size
LONGHORN or MEDIUM CHEDDAR CHEESE, grated

Cover half of each tortilla with cheese, fold tortilla in half and grill in hot frying pan or microwave on high for 30 seconds. Any filling of choice may be added to the quesadilla. Allow one small or one-half large quesadilla per serving.

Spinach Quesadillas

1 pkg. (10 oz.) frozen SPINACH
1/4 cup ONION, diced
1/4 cup sharp cheddar CHEESE
6 flour TORTILLAS, 10-12 inch size
BUTTER or MARGARINE, softened

Cook spinach according to package directions. Drain thoroughly, pressing out any excess water. In a small bowl, combine spinach, onion and cheese. Place spinach mixture on half of each tortilla, distributed equally. Fold tortillas in half, lightly butter each side and grill in a hot frying pan until slightly browned on each side.

Serves 4-6.

Zucchini Sticks

3 ZUCCHINI SQUASH
1 cup MEXICAN MAYONNAISE (see p. 32)
1 Tbsp. TABASCO® SAUCE

Cut ends from squash. Slice each squash into 12 pieces lengthwise. Mix Mexican mayonnaise and Tabasco in a small bowl. Place zucchini slices in small dish, pour mayonnaise mix over squash. Cover with foil and refrigerate. Allow to marinate for 2-3 hours.

Cheese Crisp

FLOUR TORTILLAS, any size
BUTTER
yellow or white CHEESE, grated

Spread tortilla lightly with butter. Place under broiler until butter is slightly browned. Remove from oven. Sprinkle entire surface of tortilla liberally with cheese. Place under broiler again until cheese is bubbly.

Top with your choice of ingredients such as:

- chiles
- tomatoes
- cooked meat
- shredded lettuce
- onions
- ripe olives
- sour cream
- avocado

Nachos

Nachos can be served as appetizers, snacks or as a main meal. They are a great way to use up leftovers. Build them any way you like.

CORN or TORTILLA CHIPS
LONGHORN or MEDIUM CHEDDAR CHEESE, grated

Basic Nachos:

Cover baking pan with double layer of chips, either homemade or packaged. Cover chips liberally with grated cheese. Microwave or broil until cheese melts.

Try these popular additions:

- green chiles or jalapeños
- cooked meats
- black beans
- black olives
- diced onions
- frijoles (refried beans)

Garnish with:

- chopped avocado
- diced tomatoes
- sour cream

Bean Dips

I

2 cups BEANS, (PINTO or BLACK) slightly mashed
1 can (7 oz.) diced GREEN CHILES
1 GARLIC CLOVE, crushed
1 tsp. WORCESTERSHIRE SAUCE

Combine all ingredients well. Serve warm with chips.

Makes 2 1/2 cups.

II

1 can REFRIED BEANS
1 pt. SOUR CREAM
1 cup SALSA

Combine all ingredients. Serve warm or chilled with chips.

Makes 4 cups.

III

This is especially attractive served with blue corn chips.

2 cans (15 oz. each) BLACK BEANS
3 Tbsp. OLIVE OIL
1 cup LONGHORN CHEESE, grated
1 can (4 oz.) diced GREEN CHILES, drained
1 tsp. CHILI POWDER

Drain black beans, reserving the liquid. Heat oil in a medium skillet, add beans and mash them slightly, adding the reserved bean liquid, a tablespoon at a time, to make beans easy to stir. Add cheese, chiles and chili powder and continue stirring until cheese melts. Serve warm, or in a fondue pot, with chips.

Makes 2 cups.

Chile Cheese

8 oz. CREAM CHEESE, plain, pimento or chive
1 can (4 oz.) diced GREEN CHILES or 1 can (4 oz.) diced
   JALAPEÑO CHILES

Soften cream cheese and blend in chiles of choice, green chiles for mild, jalapeños for hotter or a combination depending upon your taste.

Makes 1 cup.

Dip or Salad Dressing

1/2 cup MAYONNAISE (Do not use salad dressing)
1 can (4 oz.) diced GREEN CHILES
4 GREEN ONIONS, diced
1/2 lb. JACK CHEESE, shredded
1/2 cup plain YOGURT

Combine all ingredients except yogurt. Place in small bowl and microwave 5 minutes on medium. Stir in yogurt.

Serve warm with chips or as a warm salad dressing over chicken salad.

Makes about 2 cups.

Spicy Dip

1 pt. SOUR CREAM
1 can (4 oz.) diced GREEN CHILES
1 envelope TACO SEASONING MIX

Combine and refrigerate overnight for thorough blending of flavors.

Makes 2 1/2 cups.

Chorizo Cheese Dip

1 pkg. (12 oz.) CHORIZO
1 pkg. (1 lb.) Mexican style VELVEETA®
1 can (14 1/2 oz.) TOMATOES, chopped

Sauté chorizo until cooked. Drain well. Melt cheese in microwave. Combine chorizo, melted cheese and tomatoes. Serve with chips.

Makes about 3 cups.

Nogales Cheese Dip

In addition to being a wonderful dip, this is also a great topping for meatloaf.

1 lb. PROCESSED CHEESE
4 EGGS, hard-boiled
1 can (7 oz.) diced GREEN CHILES
1 jar (3 oz.) PIMENTOS, diced

Melt cheese. Mash eggs, add to melted cheese. Stir in chiles and pimentos. Store in refrigerator for 48 hours to blend flavors.

Makes 2 1/2 cups.

Double Dip

This is a favorite every time it is served so make plenty.

1 lb. creamed COTTAGE CHEESE
1 can (4 oz.) diced GREEN CHILES
1 Tbsp. ONION, diced
1 1/2 cup LONGHORN or MEDIUM CHEDDAR
    CHEESE, grated
1 pkg. (3 oz.) CREAM CHEESE with chives, softened
1 tsp. SUGAR
1 tsp. DRY MUSTARD

Combine cottage cheese, chiles and onion in a medium mixing bowl and blend well. Stir in grated cheese, cream cheese, sugar and dry mustard. Serve with chips or crackers.

Makes 3 cups.

Quick Chili Dip

2 cans (16 oz.) CHILI CON CARNE with beans, mild or hot
2 Tbsp. ONIONS, chopped
2 tsp. dried CILANTRO
2 Tbsp. RED WINE

Place all ingredients in a blender or food processor and blend until smooth. Serve with chips or raw vegetables.

Makes 2 cups.

Note: Depending upon the moisture content of the canned chili con carne, more wine may be needed to achieve "dipping" consistency.

Mild or hot, fresh or dried, CHILES are the most common ingredient of Mexican cuisine.

Quick and Easy Salsa

3 med. TOMATOES, diced
1 sm. GREEN CHILE, seeded and diced
1/4 cup ONION, diced
1/8 tsp. SALT

Combine and chill well.

Makes 1 cup.

Everyday Salsa

5 lg. TOMATOES, chopped
1/2 bunch CILANTRO, chopped
1/3 cup GREEN ONIONS, chopped
1 1/2 Tbsp. JALAPEÑO, seeded and diced
1 Tbsp. LIME JUICE
SALT and PEPPER to taste

Combine all ingredients and refrigerate.

Makes 3 cups.

All Canned Salsa

1 can (15 oz.) whole TOMATOES, drained
1 can (8 oz.) TOMATO SAUCE
1 can (4 oz.) diced GREEN CHILES, drained
1 Tbsp. crushed RED PEPPERS (from jar)
2 GARLIC CLOVES, crushed
1 Tbsp. dried CILANTRO
1 tsp. RED WINE VINEGAR

Mix all ingredients and store in refrigerator. This salsa stores well and can be frozen.

Makes 3 cups.

Late Day Salsa

2 lg. TOMATOES, diced
1/4 cup ONION, diced
1/2 cup CUCUMBER, diced
1/2 cup CILANTRO, diced
1 Tbsp. JALAPEÑO, seeded and diced
1 Tbsp. LIME or LEMON JUICE

Combine all ingredients and serve at room temperature. A zucchini or yellow crookneck squash may be substituted for the cucumber.

Makes about 1 cup.

Basic Salsa

4 med. TOMATOES, chopped
1 can (4 oz.) diced GREEN CHILES, drained
1/4 cup ONION, chopped
1/4 cup CILANTRO LEAVES, chopped
1/8 tsp. SALT

Combine all ingredients in a medium bowl. This salsa can be served either chilled or at room temperature.

Makes 1 1/2 cups.

Mexican Mayonnaise

1 cup MAYONNAISE
1 Tbsp. CHILI POWDER
1 tsp. dried CILANTRO

Combine ingredients and mix well.

Easy Mexican Seasoning

This is sensational sprinkled on all Mexican foods as well as on broiled meats and salads.

1/3 cup CHILI POWDER
2 Tbsp. each:
   dried CILANTRO LEAVES
   ground CUMIN
   dried OREGANO LEAVES
   dried SWEET BASIL LEAVES
1 Tbsp. each:
   GARLIC POWDER
   dried THYME LEAVES

Combine all the ingredients and store in an airtight glass jar in refrigerator. Discard after 4 months as the flavor fades.

Makes 1 cup mix.

Sandwich Spread

1 pkg. (8 oz.) CREAM CHEESE
1 can (7 oz.) diced GREEN CHILES, drained
1/4 tsp. GARLIC SALT
1/4 tsp. ONION SALT
LEFTOVER MEAT (optional), chopped

Soften cream cheese, combine with remaining ingredients. Store in refrigerator.

Makes 1 1/4 cups, without meat.

Chile Pie Crust

Line pie pan with prepared **pie crust**. Drain 1 can (4 oz.) of diced **green chiles**. Sprinkle chiles evenly over pie crust. Press into crust with back of a fork and bake according to package directions.

Mexican Marinade

1/2 cup VEGETABLE or OLIVE OIL
1 tsp. CHILI POWDER
1/2 tsp. ground PEPPER
1 tsp. dried ITALIAN SEASONING
1/2 tsp. GARLIC POWDER

Combine all ingredients and store in refrigerator. Use as a marinade for meats and vegetables.

Makes about 1/2 cup.

Meat & Poultry Marinade

3 Tbsp. OLIVE OIL
1 Tbsp. LIME JUICE
1/8 tsp. GARLIC POWDER
2/3 cup TEQUILA

Combine ingredients and blend well. Store in refrigerator in a glass container.

This is not only a delicious marinade but is equally good for basting.

CHILE OR CHILI?
Chile is the Spanish spelling and refers to the plant and pods. Chili refers to a specific recipe such as Chili con Carne.

Soups & Salads

Black Bean Soup

1 can BLACK BEAN SOUP
1/2 can WATER
1/4 cup SHERRY
1 can (4 oz.) diced GREEN CHILES, undrained
SOUR CREAM, if desired

Combine all ingredients, except sour cream, and heat in microwave 1 to 2 minutes or until hot. Top with sour cream if desired.

Serves 2.

Gazpacho

Gazpacho is a delicious vegetable soup that is served cold. The vegetables used vary from day to day, depending on what is available, so there is no standard "recipe" for gazpacho. But everyone agrees it must be "icy" cold.

2 cups TOMATO JUICE
2 TOMATOES, diced
2 cups BEEF BOUILLON
8 GREEN ONIONS, chopped
1 BELL PEPPER, any color, seeded and diced
2 sm. or 1 lg. CUCUMBER, seeded, peeled and diced
1/2 cup CELERY, diced
1 can (15 oz.) WHOLE KERNEL CORN, drained
1 JALAPEÑO, seeded and diced
1 Tbsp. dried CILANTRO
1 tsp. SUGAR
SOUR CREAM
OLIVES

Combine all ingredients and chill several hours or overnight. Top with spoonful of sour cream and sliced ripe olives.

Serves 4.

Spicy Bean Soup

A great soup on a cold night that can be made in a crockpot on low all day or in a hurry at night.

1 can (15 oz.) **PINTO BEANS**, drained
1 can (16 oz.) **TOMATOES**, undrained
1 can **BEEF BOUILLON**
1 tsp. **CHILI POWDER**
1 tsp. **GARLIC SALT**
1 tsp. dried minced **ONION**
1 tsp. dried **CHIVES**
1/2 cup dried **VEGETABLE FLAKES**

Combine all ingredients and cook as you choose—either crockpot or top of stove. If top of stove method, bring to a boil, reduce heat and simmer for 30 minutes.

Serves 4.

Pinto Bean Soup

1 cup dry **PINTO BEANS**
cold **WATER**
2 cups **HAM**, diced
1 med. **ONION**, sliced into thin rings
1 lg. or 2 med. **CARROTS**, diced
GARLIC PEPPER, to taste
1 cup **TOMATO JUICE**

Soak beans overnight in cold water. Discard water, pick over beans, discard extraneous material. In a large pan, place beans with enough fresh, cold water to cover. Bring to a boil, simmer for 2 hours. Add remaining ingredients and simmer for 3 to 4 hours. Serve with croutons and sprigs of fresh cilantro, if desired.

Serves 6.

Posole

3 Tbsp. OLIVE OIL
1 med. white ONION, diced
1 tsp. GARLIC SALT
1 1/2 lb. ground PORK (or 3/4 lb. ground PORK and
    3/4 lb. ground BEEF)
1 tsp. ground CUMIN
1 tsp. ground OREGANO
1 can (15 oz.) HOMINY, undrained

Heat oil in large skillet. Add onion, garlic salt, ground meat, cumin and oregano. Sauté over medium heat until meat is thoroughly cooked and the onions are lightly browned. Add hominy, cover skillet and simmer for 30 minutes. Serve in bowls with topping of choice such as sour cream, guacamole or tortilla strips.

Serves 6.

*Cumin is a seasoning commonly used
in Mexican cooking and gives
a distinctive warm flavor to many foods.*

Albondigas

(Meatball Soup)

1 lb. lean ground ROUND STEAK
6 GREEN ONIONS, sliced in 1/8 inch pieces
1 tsp. GARLIC PEPPER
1/2 tsp. crushed RED PEPPERS, from jar
1/2 tsp. ground ALLSPICE
3 cans (10 oz. each) BEEF CONSOMME
2 med. TOMATOES, diced
2 med. ZUCCHINI, diced
1 cup CABBAGE, thinly sliced
2 ears CORN, cut into 1/4 inch pieces

In large mixing bowl, combine ground round steak, onions, garlic pepper, red peppers and allspice. Form into balls about 1 inch in diameter. Empty consomme into large saucepan or dutch oven and heat to the boiling point. Gently place meatballs, one at a time, into the boiling consomme. Add tomatoes, zucchini, cabbage and corn. Reduce heat and simmer gently, uncovered, for 45 minutes.

Serves 6.

Chilled Cherry Soup

2 cans (1 lb., 4 oz. each) pitted sour CHERRIES
1 1/2 Tbsp. TAPIOCA
2/3 cup SUGAR
1/4 tsp. ground CINNAMON
1/4 cup LEMON JUICE

Combine all ingredients in a large saucepan and cook over medium low heat until mixture is thickened. Remove from heat and let cool. Serve chilled. Can be served in chilled mugs.

Serves 6.

Note: This is a great picnic soup for trips to the beach. The high country of Mexico grows all types of fruits and this soup can be made with fresh cherries. If fresh cherries are used, omit the sugar.

The basic foods of the Aztec and Mayan cultures were corn, tomatoes, chiles and beans. These are still some of the most important foods of Mexico today.

Anytime Soup

This unique soup may be served warm, at room temperature, or chilled.

8 med. RED POTATOES
1 med. ONION, sliced very thin
1 BELL PEPPER, seeded
  and diced
1 cup CARROTS, diced
1 tsp. GARLIC SALT

1 Tbsp. dried PARSLEY
  FLAKES
3/4 cup extra virgin
  OLIVE OIL
1/4 cup SWEET BASIL
  VINEGAR

Boil potatoes, cool and cut into cubes. In large bowl combine potatoes, onion, pepper, carrots, garlic salt and parsley flakes. In small bowl, mix olive oil and vinegar. Pour over potato mixture and toss gently.

Serves 6.

Tortilla & Chicken Soup

1 lg. WHITE ONION, chopped
1 can (7 oz.) diced GREEN CHILES, undrained
1 can (15 1/2 oz.) MEXICAN STYLE or STEWED TOMATOES
5 cups CHICKEN BROTH
4 cups cooked CHICKEN, diced
1 tsp. ground CUMIN
1/2 tsp. dried RED PEPPERS, from jar
2 tsp. WORCESTERSHIRE SAUCE
2 cups WHIPPING CREAM
3 lg. AVOCADOS, cubed
1 pkg. restaurant-style CORN TORTILLA STRIPS

In large kettle, gently sauté onions and chiles. When onions are slightly limp, add all other ingredients except whipping cream, avocados and chips. Cover and simmer slowly for 1-2 hours. Turn off heat and stir in cream. Place avocado in six bowls, fill bowls with soup and sprinkle with tortilla strips.

Serves 6.

Summer Citrus Salad

1 cup each ORANGE and GRAPEFRUIT SECTIONS
1 sm. RED ONION, separated into rings
2 AVOCADOS, cut into cubes
1/2 cup YOGURT, any fruit flavor
LETTUCE leaves

Combine fruit sections, onion rings and avocado in a medium bowl. Add yogurt and stir gently. Serve on lettuce leaves.

Serves 3.

*It is said that when Diaz arrived in Mexico,
he brought seven orange seeds with him.
Today oranges are one of Mexico's
most common fruits.*

Montezuma Salad

2 AVOCADOS   1 Tbsp. LIME JUICE
1 TOMATO   1 JALAPEÑO, seeded
1 ONION   and chopped
1 BELL PEPPER   LETTUCE LEAVES

Chop all ingredients about the same size. Sprinkle with lime juice. Serve on lettuce leaves.

Serves 3.

Avocado Salad

2 TOMATOES, chopped
2 AVOCADOS, chopped
1/4 cup prepared SALSA
2 Tbsp. dark RUM

1 Tbsp. LIME JUICE
ground PEPPER, to taste
LETTUCE leaves

Combine tomatoes, avocados, salsa, rum and lime juice. Toss gently. Add pepper to taste and serve on lettuce.

Serves 4.

Chile Salad

3 TOMATOES, chopped
1 lg. can sliced BLACK OLIVES, drained
6 GREEN ONIONS, cut in 1/2 inch pieces
1 can (7 oz.) whole GREEN CHILES, sliced
1 cup GARLIC CROUTONS
4 Tbsp. OLIVE OIL
2 Tbsp. WHITE WINE VINEGAR
LETTUCE LEAVES

Combine all ingredients except lettuce and chill. Serve on lettuce leaves.

Serves 4.

Taco Salad

4 cups TORTILLA CHIPS
1 lb. ground BEEF or ground TURKEY, cooked and drained
1 can (15 oz.) BLACK BEANS or KIDNEY BEANS, drained
1 small ONION, sliced thin into rings
1 1/2 cup LONGHORN CHEESE, grated
1 cup LETTUCE, shredded
2 med. TOMATOES, cut into quarters
1 cup sliced BLACK OLIVES, drained
2 med. AVOCADOS, sliced

Place one cup of chips on each of four salad plates. In large bowl, combine cooked meat, beans and onion and toss well. Place equal amounts on the chips and top each salad with cheese, lettuce, tomatoes, olives and avocado slices. Serve with Cilantro Cream Topping (see p. 74).

Serves 4.

Corn Salad

1 can (15 oz.) whole kernel CORN, drained
1 can (4 oz.) diced GREEN CHILES, drained
1 can (8 oz.) sliced pickled BEETS, drained
6 GREEN ONIONS, cut into 1/2 inch pieces
1/2 cup BELL PEPPER, any color, chopped
2 med. TOMATOES, chopped
1/8 tsp. flavored PEPPER, freshly ground
1/4 cup WHITE WINE VINEGAR
1/2 cup OLIVE OIL
LETTUCE LEAVES

Combine all ingredients except lettuce leaves in medium bowl. Toss well. Chill until ready to serve. Serve on lettuce leaves.

Serves 6.

Potato Salad

1 lb. NEW POTATOES (RED), cooked and diced
1 can (15 oz.) GREEN BEANS, drained
1 sm. ONION, diced
1/3 cup CELERY, diced
1/3 cup BELL PEPPER, diced, any color
1 cup CABBAGE, finely shredded
1/2 cup RADISHES, sliced
1/2 cup fresh CILANTRO, chopped
1/2 CUCUMBER, seeded, peeled and diced
1/2 cup OLIVE OIL
1/3 cup LIME JUICE

In large bowl, combine all ingredients except oil and lime juice. Chill well. In small bowl, using wire whisk, beat lime juice into olive oil and pour over potato salad just before serving.

Serves 6.

Baja Shrimp Salad

1 lb. SHRIMP, cooked, deveined and peeled,
    cut in bite-sized pieces
1 CUCUMBER, peeled, seeded and sliced very thin
12 RADISHES, sliced thin
4 GREEN ONIONS, cut in 1/2 inch pieces
1/2 cup WHITE WINE VINEGAR
1 Tbsp. SUGAR

In medium bowl, combine all ingredients and toss well. Best when served chilled.

Serves 4.

Chicken & Avocado Salad

1 cup cooked CHICKEN, cubed
1 AVOCADO, cubed
1 med. TOMATO, chopped
1 tsp. LEMON JUICE
1 Tbsp. SALSA
SOUR CREAM

Toss all ingredients together and serve on lettuce leaves. Top with sour cream, if desired.

Serves 2.

Vegetable Salad

1 cup raw CAULIFLOWER, sliced
1 cup raw BROCCOLI, cut into large flowerettes
1 ZUCCHINI, quartered and cut into 1/2-inch sections
1 BELL PEPPER, seeded and diced
10 RADISHES, sliced
1 CUCUMBER, quartered and cut into 1/2-inch sections
PARMESAN CHEESE, if desired
SALAD DRESSING of choice

Serve with Mexican Mayonnaise (see p. 32)

Combine cauliflower, broccoli, zucchini, bell pepper, radishes and cucumber in a large bowl. Serve in bowls and add dressing and Parmesan cheese as desired.

Serves 6.

Pinto Bean Salad

1 can (15 oz.) PINTO BEANS, drained
1/3 cup OLIVE OIL
2 Tbsp. VINEGAR
1 can (4 oz.) sliced BLACK OLIVES, drained
1 can (4 oz.) diced GREEN CHILES, drained
6 GREEN ONIONS, cut in 1/2-inch pieces
Fresh cracked PEPPER, if desired
1/2 head LETTUCE, shredded

Combine all ingredients in a large bowl and toss well. Chill for an hour until all ingredients are cold.

Serves 4.

Yucatan Salad

3 Tbsp. OLIVE OIL
3 tsp. WHITE WINE VINEGAR
1 lg. or 2 med. AVOCADOS, cubed
1 can (15 oz.) BLACK BEANS, drained
1 can (8 oz.) whole kernel CORN, drained
1 jar (3 oz.) PIMENTOS, diced
1 can (16 oz.) PINEAPPLE slices, drained
LETTUCE leaves

Combine olive oil and vinegar in a medium bowl. Add avocados, beans, corn and pimentos and toss lightly. Arrange pineapple slices on lettuce leaves, top with avocado, bean, corn mixture.

Note: This salad is also delicious made with poppy seed salad dressing.

Serves 4.

Sonoran Salad

1 can (28 oz.) RANCH BEANS, drained
1 lg. or 2 med. TOMATOES, chopped
8 GREEN ONIONS, cut in 1-inch pieces, including some tops
2 cups LETTUCE, shredded
1 cup LONGHORN CHEESE, grated
RANCH SALAD DRESSING

Combine beans, tomatoes, onions, lettuce and cheese in a large bowl. Add desired amount of dressing. Chill well.
Serves 4.

Tres Bean Salad

1 can (15 oz.) each PINTO BEANS, BLACK BEANS and
    KIDNEY BEANS, drained
1 can (7 oz.) diced GREEN CHILES, drained
4 GREEN ONIONS, cut in 1/2-inch pieces
1 cup yellow or white CHEESE, cubed
1 Tbsp. crushed RED PEPPERS (from jar)
1 pt. SOUR CREAM

Combine all ingredients and serve in salad bowls.
Serves 4.

Black Bean Salad

1 can (15 oz.) BLACK BEANS, drained
3 EGGS, hard boiled, chopped
1/3 cup RED ONION, chopped
1/2 cup LONGHORN CHEDDAR CHEESE, cubed
1/2 head LETTUCE

Combine ingredients in medium bowl. When ready to serve, toss with salad dressing of choice. Serve on bed of lettuce.
Serves 4.

Salad Marinada

*This marinade is so simple and the results are amazing. Accord-
ing to the story passed down to the author of this book, this
marinade extended the life of garden vegetables and made a
delicious snack on a hot day. When making a salad, vegetables
were lifted out of the marinade bowl and added to the salad.
Every week or so, the marinade was disposed of and a new
supply prepared. Almost any vegetable benefits from time in the
marinade.*

1 1/2 cups WATER   2 Tbsp. SUGAR
1/2 cup VINEGAR   2 shakes of SALT

This makes 2 cups of marinade.   Change amounts for
individual needs. Keep refrigerated.

Some suggested vegetables:

- cucumbers
- radishes
- onion rings
- zucchini

- chiles
- bell peppers
- carrots
- mushrooms

Tostada Topping

1 cup COTTAGE CHEESE
6 Tbsp. MILK
1 Tbsp. LEMON or LIME JUICE
1 tsp. CHILI POWDER

Combine ingredients in blender. Blend on high speed to
liquefy. Store in refrigerator. To serve, dollop on top of tostadas.

Makes 1 1/4 cups.

Cancún Salad Dressing

This delightfully different salad dressing may be kept on hand all the time. It is equally suitable for salads or as a marinade.

1/2 cup OLIVE OIL
1/2 cup LIME JUICE
3 Tbsp. WINE VINEGAR
2 Tbsp. crushed RED PEPPERS (dried, from jar)

Combine all ingredients and store in refrigerator in a glass jar.

Makes 1 1/4 cups.

Guadalajara Honey Cream Dressing

This delicious dressing is wonderful not only as a salad dressing but as a dip for fresh fruit served as a dessert.

2 EGGS
1/4 cup HONEY
1/4 cup LEMON JUICE
1 cup WHIPPING CREAM

Beat eggs until fluffy. Add honey and lemon juice. Cook over medium heat until thickened. Let cool 5 minutes, fold in cream. Chill well.

Makes about 2 1/2 cups.

Mexico City was once known as Tenochtitlan and was the pride of the Aztecs in the 14th and 15th centuries. Then, as now, it is one of the largest cities in the world.

Canyon Broiled Grapefruit

This is delicious served as a dessert or as a first course in place of salads.

1 GRAPEFRUIT
1/3 cup SUGAR
1/3 cup cream SHERRY

Cut grapefruit in half, sprinkle equal amounts of sugar and sherry on each half.

Place under broiler for about 5 minutes or until lightly browned.

Serves 2.

Grapefruit, called TORONJA in Spanish, is a member of the immensely popular family of citrus fruits found throughout Mexico. It is said that oranges were a gift from Mexico to California several centuries ago. In addition to grapefruit and oranges, the lemons and limes of Mexico are among the world's best and all citrus fruits are used extensively in the cuisine of Mexico.

Breads

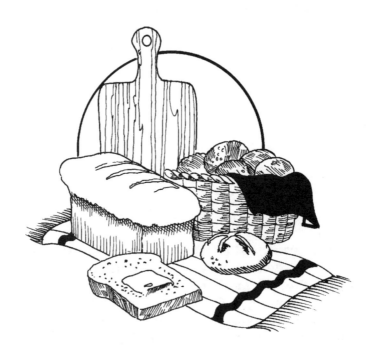

Biscuits with Chile Butter

To make chile butter: Blend one cup (1/2 pound) of **butter** with one 4 ounce can of **diced green chiles** that have been well drained.

Select any packaged biscuits. Spread with chile butter and bake as directed on the package.

Note: For those who want a "hotter" chile butter, add 1 teaspoon **red chili powder** to the butter mix.

The predominant language of Mexico is Mexican Spanish, which is unlike the Castilian Spanish, the official language of Spain. In addition, there are more than 50 Indian languages spoken in the country.

Chile Bread

1 loaf ITALIAN or FRENCH BREAD, unsliced
1 stick BUTTER, melted
1 can (4 oz.) diced GREEN CHILES, drained
1/2 cup CHEESE, grated

Slice bread almost all the way through. Combine melted butter, chiles and cheese and spread between bread slices. Place loaf on plate and cover with paper towel. Microwave on 50% power until cheese melts.

Chile Corn Bread

1 package CORN BREAD MIX
1 sm. can CREAMED CORN
1 can (7 oz.) whole GREEN CHILES, drained
1 cup LONGHORN or CHEDDAR CHEESE, grated

Prepare corn bread mix according to package directions, adding the creamed corn to batter. Pour one-half of mixture into a medium size greased baking pan. Place a layer of one-half of the chiles and one-half of the cheese on mixture. Pour remaining batter into pan, top with remaining chiles and cheese. Bake as directed on package.

Banana Bread

1/3 cup SHORTENING
1 cup SUGAR
1/2 cup SOUR MILK or BUTTERMILK
2 EGGS, beaten
2 cups FLOUR
1 tsp. BAKING SODA
2 ripe BANANAS, mashed

Cream together shortening and sugar. Add remaining ingredients, in the order listed. Bake in a lightly greased loaf pan in a 350 degree oven for one hour. Cool, turn out on plate and let cool again before slicing.

Jalapeño Cheese Rolls

1 pkg. CRESCENT ROLLS (from dairy case) any brand,
   10-12 rolls
1 cup LONGHORN or MEDIUM CHEDDAR CHEESE, grated
1 jar pickled JALAPEÑO slices, drained

In the center of each roll place 3 jalapeño slices. Top with cheese. Roll dough and bake according to package directions.

Allow 2-3 rolls per person.

Main Dishes

Chicken Tortilla Bake

1 med. (10-12 oz.) bag CORN TORTILLA CHIPS
4 cups cooked CHICKEN or TURKEY, cubed
1 can (10 1/2 oz.) CREAM OF CHICKEN SOUP
1 can (7 oz.) diced GREEN CHILES, undrained
1 bunch GREEN ONIONS, cut in 1/2-inch pieces with tops
2 cups LONGHORN or COLBY CHEESE, grated
1 can (2 1/2 oz.) sliced BLACK OLIVES

Place one-half of the tortilla chips in the bottom of a medium baking dish. Set aside. In a large bowl, combine chicken (or turkey), soup, chiles, onions and cheese. Place half of this mixture over the chips, cover with remaining chips and finish with the remaining chicken mixture. Microwave on high for 5 minutes or bake in a 375 degree oven for 20 minutes or until bubbly hot. Top with black olives.

Serves 4.

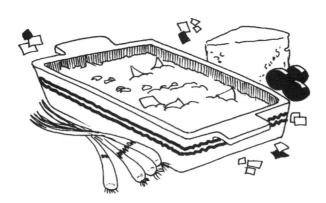

Mucho Nachos

2 cups leftover CHICKEN or TURKEY, cut into
    bite-size pieces
1 can (8 oz.) whole kernel CORN, drained
1 can (8 oz.) BLACK BEANS, drained
1/2 cup SALSA
1/2 cup MAYONNAISE
1 tsp. dried RED PEPPERS, crushed
1 cup LONGHORN CHEESE, shredded
3 cups TORTILLA CHIPS

In a large bowl, combine chicken or turkey, corn, beans, salsa, mayonnaise, peppers and 3/4 cup of the cheese. Layer a baking dish with 2 cups of the chips, cover with mixture from the bowl and top with remaining cheese and the other cup of chips. Microwave on high for about three minutes or until hot and bubbly.

Serves 5-6.

Hurry Up Tamale Meal

Tamales are so delicious that they are now enjoyed all year instead of just on special holidays. Although they are not difficult to make, they are time consuming, so this recipe provides a delicious tamale meal in a hurry.

8 frozen TAMALES, any variety
2 cups cooked CHICKEN, diced
1 bunch GREEN ONIONS, sliced into 1-inch pieces
1 1/2 cups LONGHORN or JACK CHEESE, shredded
SALSA

Prepare tamales in microwave or oven as directed on package. Place 2 tamales on each plate, distribute chicken, onions and cheese evenly over tamales. Heat until cheese melts. Serve with salsa.

Serves 4.

Chorizo con Huevos

This makes a delightful brunch or supper.

1 lb. CHORIZO, cooked and drained well
8 lg. EGGS
1/4 cup MILK
1/8 tsp. ground ALLSPICE
SALT and PEPPER, to taste

Fry chorizo in a medium skillet until thoroughly cooked. Drain in a colander, leaving the skillet with any leftover bits. Set skillet and chorizo aside. Beat eggs, milk and allspice. Return skillet to stove over medium high heat. Add eggs, waiting for one minute, then add chorizo and scramble together until eggs are cooked. Salt and pepper to taste.

Serves 4.

Tostada Basics

A tostada is an open-face Mexican sandwich. It can be made from either corn or flour tortillas, although corn tortillas are most commonly used. If flour tortillas are used, choose either the six inch or fajita size. To crisp the tortilla, heat about one-half inch of vegetable oil in a small skillet. Fry the tortilla until crispy, turning with tongs. Drain flat on paper towels.

Shrimp Tostadas

This is a summer favorite using the delicious shrimp from Mexican waters. Other seafood, such as lobster or scallops, may be substituted for shrimp.

4 prepared CORN TORTILLAS
20 lg. SHRIMP, cooked and peeled with tails removed
1 Tbsp. LIME JUICE
1 can (15 oz.) BLACK BEANS, drained
4 sm. TOMATOES, cut into quarters
2 cups LETTUCE, shredded
4 Tbsp. SOUR CREAM
SALSA

On each tortilla, arrange 5 shrimp in a circle. Sprinkle with lime juice. Sprinkle black beans, equally divided, over shrimp. Arrange tomato quarters on each serving, top with lettuce and a tablespoon of sour cream per tostada. Serve with salsa.

Serves 4.

Chicken with Black Beans

4 cooked CHICKEN breasts or thighs and drumsticks
1 can (15 oz.) BLACK BEANS, drained
1/2 cup SALSA
1/2 cup WHITE WINE
1/2 tsp. ALLSPICE

Place cooked chicken pieces on four dinner plates. Combine black beans, salsa, wine and allspice in a medium bowl and blend well. Top each serving of chicken with bean mixture, equally divided among the four servings. If further heating is required, place in microwave for 30 seconds on highest power.

Serves 4.

Sloppy Josés

1 1/2 lb. lean GROUND BEEF
1 can (15 oz.) REFRIED BEANS
1 med. ONION, chopped
1 GARLIC CLOVE, crushed
1 can (7 oz.) diced GREEN CHILES or one JALAPEÑO,
    seeded and diced
1 tsp. CHILI POWDER
1/2 cup BEER
1 cup SALSA
6 HAMBURGER BUNS

Sauté ground beef until browned. Drain, if necessary. Combine beef and all other ingredients, except buns, in a large saucepan and simmer for 15 minutes. Split buns, allowing a top and bottom per serving. Spoon beef mixture evenly over buns.

Serves 6.

Tamale Balls

1 can (15 oz.) TAMALES, drained
1 lb. lean GROUND
   BEEF
1/4 cup plain BREAD
   CRUMBS
SALSA

Mash tamales in a medium bowl. Sauté ground beef until thoroughly cooked. Drain well. Combine tamales, beef and bread crumbs. Form into 1-inch balls and place on large baking pan. Bake in 350 degree oven for about 10 minutes or until hot. Serve with salsa.

Makes about 36 balls.

Quickie Turkey Chili

2 cans (15 oz. each) meatless CHILI WITH BEANS
2 cups leftover TURKEY or 1 lb. ground TURKEY, cooked
1/2 cup CHEESE, grated
1/4 cup ONION, diced

Empty canned chili into a medium saucepan. Add turkey and heat. Serve in individual bowls and top with cheese and onions.

Serves 4.

Red Chili Stew

4 cups cooked MEAT, cubed
2 cans (15 oz. each) ENCHILADA SAUCE
1/4 tsp. GARLIC POWDER
1/4 tsp. ONION POWDER
1 Tbsp. dried PARSLEY FLAKES
2 cans (15 oz. each) PINTO or BLACK BEANS, drained
cooked RICE, if desired

Combine all ingredients, except the rice, in a large saucepan. Simmer until piping hot. Serve in bowls, over rice, if desired.

Serves 4.

Spanish Chicken

2 Tbsp. LIME JUICE
1 tsp. dried CILANTRO
1 tsp. CHILI POWDER
1 tsp. OLIVE OIL
4 boneless CHICKEN BREASTS

Combine lime juice, cilantro, chili powder and olive oil. Place chicken in a large frying pan and pour mixture over chicken. Cook over medium-high heat, turning chicken once, until chicken is done. Serve with pan drippings.

Serves 4.

Swordfish con Salsa

4 SWORDFISH STEAKS (about 1 lb.)
2/3 cup OLIVE OIL
8 GREEN ONIONS, minced with some tops
1/3 cup LIME JUICE
1 Tbsp. diced GREEN CHILES or sliced JALAPEÑO,
    both canned
1/2 bunch fresh CILANTRO, chopped
freshly cracked LEMON PEPPER, to taste

Cook fish, either broiled or baked, until done. To make the salsa, combine oil, onions, lime juice, chiles or jalapeños, and cilantro in a medium bowl and mix well. Serve fish with salsa.

Serves 4.

Flauta Basics

The word flauta means flute in Spanish and is used to describe a flute-shaped, or rolled, taco. Flautas may be made with either corn or flour tortillas, however, corn tortillas are the most commonly used. If preparing flautas with corn tortillas, heat the tortillas for a few seconds in an ungreased frying pan to make them flexible and easy to roll.

To assemble flautas, place a small amount of selected filling down the center of the tortilla. Roll the tortilla tightly and secure with a wooden toothpick. Flautas are now ready for cooking. Fry in one-half inch of vegetable oil until crispy. Remove toothpick before serving.

Chicken Flautas

12 corn TORTILLAS
VEGETABLE OIL
2 cups cooked CHICKEN, diced
1/4 cup ONION, diced
1 small GREEN CHILE, seeded and diced

Prepare tortillas as described above. Combine chicken, onion and green chile. Spoon equal amounts of mixture down the center of each tortilla and roll tightly, securing with a toothpick. Fry each flauta in hot oil until golden brown, turning with tongs. Drain on paper towels.

Allow 2-3 flautas per serving.

Chili Tamale Supreme

1 can (15 oz.) TAMALES
1 can (15 oz.) CHILI CON CARNE, with or without beans
CHEESE, grated
ONION, chopped

Mash tamales with fork, add chili and mix well. Place in casserole and sprinkle with grated cheese and chopped onion, if desired. Microwave on high, covered loosely, for 5 minutes or until thoroughly heated.

Serves 4.

*Ristras, strings of red chiles, are believed to
ward off evil spirits. Ristras are
hung by the front door.*

Minute Steaks Verde

4 MINUTE STEAKS
FLOUR
VEGETABLE OIL
1 can (4 oz.) diced GREEN CHILES
1/2 cup CHEESE, grated

Flour steaks lightly and brown in hot vegetable oil. Drain on paper towels. Transfer to baking pan, cover each steak with equal amounts of chiles and cheese. Bake at 350 degrees or microwave on medium power until cheese is bubbly.

Serves 4.

Quick Weekend Chili Pie

This easy casserole dinner can be prepared ahead and baked when convenient.

1 Tbsp. OLIVE OIL
2 lbs. lean GROUND BEEF
1 med. ONION, chopped
2 GARLIC CLOVES, crushed
1 1/2 Tbsp. CHILI POWDER
1 tsp. dried CILANTRO
1/2 tsp. dried OREGANO
1/2 tsp. dried BASIL
1 can (15 oz.) TOMATOES, drained
1 can (15 oz.) PINTO BEANS, drained
1 can (7 oz.) diced GREEN CHILES, undrained
1/2 cup RED WINE
1 pkg. CORN BREAD MIX
1 EGG
1/4 cup MILK
1 sm. can CREAMED CORN
1/2 cup LONGHORN CHEESE, grated

Sauté beef, onion and garlic in oil until beef is browned. Add chili powder, cilantro, oregano, basil, tomatoes, beans, chiles and wine. Simmer together 15 minutes. While simmering, combine corn bread mix, egg, milk and corn. Place meat mixture in large casserole and top with corn bread mix. Sprinkle cheese on top. Bake in a 350 degree oven for 45 minutes.

Serves 8.

Mexican Hamburgers

1 lb. lean GROUND BEEF
1/4 cup flavored BREAD CRUMBS
1 Tbsp. GREEN ONION, minced
1 Tbsp. SALSA

Combine and shape into four patties. Cook as desired.

Serves 4.

Mexi-Cheeseburgers

1 lb. ground BEEF
1 can (4 oz.) diced GREEN CHILES
1/2 cup cheddar CHEESE, grated
1/4 cup ONIONS, diced

Combine all ingredients in a medium bowl. Shape into 6 patties. Grill outside or broil in oven to desired doneness.

Serves 6.

Easy Chili

1 lb. GROUND BEEF
1 can PINTO or BLACK BEANS, drained
1 med. ONION, chopped
1 can TOMATO PUREE
1 GARLIC CLOVE, crushed
2 Tbsp. CHILI POWDER or 1 Tbsp. CHILE POWDER
1 Tbsp. ground CUMIN
1/4 tsp. ALLSPICE

Brown ground beef, drain any excess fat. Add remaining ingredients and simmer together for 15 minutes or longer, if desired. After preparation, the chili mixture can also be kept warm in a crockpot.

Serves 4.

Mexico is a multifaceted land of deserts, mountains, forests and cities that covers approximately 780,000 square miles and has almost 6000 miles of coast line.

Carne Asada

2 lbs. SIRLOIN STEAK, cut into 4 serving size pieces
1/2 tsp. dried CILANTRO
1/4 tsp. ground CUMIN
1/4 tsp. ground ALLSPICE
2 Tbsp. LIME JUICE
1 can (7 oz.) diced GREEN CHILES, undrained

Place steak in ovenproof baking dish. In a small bowl, combine all other ingredients and spread evenly over the steak. Bake, covered, for 3-4 hours in a 325 degree oven.

Serves 4.

Taco Basics

Tacos are probably the most popular and best known of Mexican foods. A traditional taco is made from a corn tortilla that is folded into a half-moon shape and deep fried. To prepare taco shells in this way, heat one-half inch of vegetable oil in a small frying pan. Using tongs, dip the tortilla into the hot oil for 5 seconds, just enough to soften the tortilla. Fold the tortilla in half and cook until crisp on each side. Drain on paper towels.

A soft taco is usually made from a flour tortilla. Select the small size flour tortillas, warm them a few seconds in a microwave or toaster oven and fill as you would the traditional tacos.

Almost any filling can be used in tacos such as meats, beans, cheeses and vegetables. Fillings are usually topped with salsa.

Almost every market sells prepared taco shells, which come in boxes of 10 or 12. These can be handy to keep on the shelf for "Instant Tacos." When purchasing fresh corn tortillas, look for soft and pliable tortillas with no cracks.

Chicken Tacos

10 TORTILLAS, corn or flour
2 cups cooked CHICKEN, chopped
1 can (4 oz.) sliced BLACK OLIVES, drained
1/2 cup CUCUMBER, peeled and diced
1/4 cup RADISHES, diced
SALSA

Prepare taco shells of choice. Combine chicken, olives, cucumber and radishes in small bowl and divide among the taco shells. Top with salsa.

Allow 2-3 tacos per serving.

Quickie Chicken Tacos

1 pkg. prepared TACO SHELLS
1 can CHICKEN CHUNKS
CHEESE, grated (longhorn, cheddar, Jack or colby)
LETTUCE, shredded
SALSA

Fill taco shells with chicken and grated cheese. Microwave on high for 45 seconds. Remove to plates, add lettuce and salsa.

Allow 2-3 tacos per serving.

Beef Tacos

Beef tacos can be made from ground beef or shredded beef.

12 CORN TORTILLAS
1 lb. GROUND BEEF, cooked
1/4 cup ONION, chopped
1 cup CHEDDAR or JACK CHEESE, grated
2 TOMATOES, chopped
2 cups LETTUCE, shredded
SALSA

Prepare tortillas as directed (see p. 69). Sauté ground beef until brown. Drain well. Fill each tortilla with cooked beef, onion, cheese, tomato and lettuce, equally distributed between the tortillas. Serve with salsa.

Allow 2-3 tacos per serving.

Black Bean Tacos

1 pkg. TACO SHELLS
1 can (14 1/2 oz.) BLACK BEANS
1/4 cup ONIONS, diced
1 can (4 oz.) diced GREEN CHILES
1 med. TOMATO, diced
SALSA

Drain black beans, place in medium size bowl and mash slightly. Add onions and chiles. Fill taco shells with bean mixture. Warm in microwave or toaster oven. Top with tomatoes. Serve with salsa.

Allow 2-3 tacos per serving.

Vegetable Tacos

12 FLOUR TORTILLAS, 6-inch diameter (sometimes called
    fajita tortillas)
1 ZUCCHINI, quartered
1/2 cup RED ONION, chopped
1 GREEN PEPPER, seeded and chopped
24 GREEN OLIVES, diced
1 TOMATO, chopped
1 Tbsp. LIME JUICE
SALSA

Warm tortillas in microwave or toaster oven. Combine zucchini, onion, green pepper, olives and tomato in a medium bowl. Sprinkle with lime juice and stir well. Spoon equal amounts of vegetable combination into tortillas. Serve with salsa.

Serves 4-6.

Tacos Frijoles

1 box TACO SHELLS
1 can (15 oz.) REFRIED BEANS
1 AVOCADO, chopped
1 1/2 cups JACK CHEESE, grated
2 cups LETTUCE, shredded
SALSA

Fill taco shells with equal amounts of beans. Warm in microwave or toaster oven. Remove to a platter and fill each with avocado, cheese and lettuce. Serve with salsa.

Serves 4.

Masa is corn flour that has been treated
and is used to make tortillas,
flat enchiladas and tamales.

Shredded Beef

Use for tacos, enchiladas, tostadas or wherever shredded beef
is used in Mexican cooking.

4-5 lbs. BEEF ROAST
1/2 cup BEEF BOUILLON
1/2 cup DRY VERMOUTH
1 BAY LEAF

Combine all ingredients in a crockpot or large dutch oven. Cover tightly. Cook in a crockpot on low for 10-12 hours or in a dutch oven for 8-10 hours on lowest simmer. Remove meat to platter. Let cool, pull meat apart, using two dinner forks. Freeze any leftover meat.

Makes 2-3 lbs. cooked meat.

Fajita Basics

The true origin of the fajita is unknown, however, the ranchers of northern Mexico marinated less tender, or left-over, beef rolled it into a tortilla and made use of whatever garnish was available. On the early ranches, before electricity was available, food had to be consumed promptly to prevent spoilage. This resulted in many of the eating customs we find in Mexico today, such as the enjoyment of many snacks and the very late dinner hour. Foods not consumed at the late night meal could be kept through the cool night to be used in a breakfast dish.

Today's fajitas are exciting, varied and fun to make. Frequently, the traditional marinated, less tender cuts of beef are served, but chicken, turkey, seafood and vegetables are also very popular. To prepare fajitas, grill onions, tomatoes and bell peppers and serve with the grilled meat, poultry or seafood or vegetables on a sizzling platter accompanied by warmed flour tortillas

Marinade por Fajitas

Whether you prefer beef, chicken, shrimp or other fajitas, this marinade will make them very special. This recipe is enough to marinate 1 pound. When making this marinade, use a non-metallic bowl.

1/2 cup bottled WATER
1/4 cup fresh LIME JUICE
1 lg. or 2 sm. GARLIC
   CLOVES, crushed
1/2 tsp. ground CUMIN

1 tsp. dried CILANTRO
1 Tbsp. VEGETABLE OIL
1 Tbsp. WORCESTERSHIRE
   SAUCE
2 tsp. BROWN SUGAR

Combine all ingredients and blend well. Marinate for at least 1 hour before cooking. This marinade can be used again and keeps well in the refrigerator.

Cilantro Cream Topping

This topping is delicious with tacos, enchiladas, rellenos, tostadas and almost any recipe using tortillas.

2 cups SOUR CREAM
1/2 bunch fresh CILANTRO

Empty sour cream into a small bowl. With scissors, finely snip cilantro into sour cream. Stir well.

Makes 2 cups.

Quick & Easy Chile Rellenos

1 can (7 oz.) whole green CHILES
1/2 lb. JACK or other white CHEESE
1 pkg. TEMPURA MIX
VEGETABLE OIL

Rinse and dry chiles, being careful not to tear them. Cut cheese into strips and place a strip in each chile. Prepare tempura mix according to package directions. Coat each stuffed chile with tempura batter and place gently, with slotted spoon, in hot oil. Fry until golden brown. Drain on paper towels.

Serves 2.

Chorizo & Yams

1 lb. CHORIZO, cooked and drained
1 lg. can (28 oz.) SWEET POTATOES or YAMS, undrained
1/3 cup CREAM
1/2 tsp. ground ALLSPICE
1/3 cup BROWN SUGAR

Drain sweet potatoes, saving juice in a small bowl. Slice potatoes and place them in a lightly buttered baking dish. Spread cooked chorizo over potatoes. To the juice, add cream and allspice and stir until thoroughly blended. Pour over potatoes and chorizo. Sprinkle top with brown sugar. Bake in a 350 degree oven for 30 minutes.

Serves 3-4.

Acapulco Shrimp

2 lbs. lg. cooked SHRIMP, shelled and deveined, with tails
    left on, chilled
1 cup CHILI SAUCE
1 Tbsp. fresh LIME JUICE
1 1/2 tsp. HORSERADISH, cream style
1/4 tsp. TABASCO® SAUCE

Clean shrimp and set aside or place in refrigerator to chill. In a small bowl, combine the remaining ingredients and stir until completely blended. Serve with shrimp. Serves 4-6.

Sonoran Style Pasta

1 pkg. (8 oz.) CREAM CHEESE
1/2 cup fresh CILANTRO, chopped
1/4 tsp. GARLIC PEPPER
1 Tbsp. OLIVE OIL
8 oz. PASTA

Place cream cheese in a medium bowl and soften in microwave. Add cilantro, garlic pepper and oil. Stir well. Set aside. In a large saucepan, bring 8 cups of water to a boil. Add a few drops of olive or vegetable oil to prevent boiling over. Add pasta and cook until done. Pour pasta into colander and rinse well under cold water to remove excess and sticky starch. When rinsed, return pasta to saucepan, add cream cheese sauce and stir well. Serve warm.

Serves 4.

Quick Spanish Rice Supper

1 pkg. SPANISH RICE MIX
1 can (4 oz.) diced GREEN CHILES, drained
6 HOT DOGS, cut in 1/2 inch pieces

Prepare Spanish rice mix according to package directions. Add hot dogs and chiles. Serve hot.

Serves 4.

Guadalajara, founded in 1539, is Mexico's second largest city. With its sixteenth century architecture, it is a city with beautiful parks, plazas and trees.

Enchilada Basics

Among Mexican favorites is the versatile enchilada. An enchilada is a corn tortilla rolled around a filling of choice and then baked. Prepare the corn tortillas by dipping into hot vegetable oil for a few seconds per side. This softens the tortillas so they don't break or crack when rolling. Drain on paper towels. Tortillas are now ready for filling.

Some enchilada recipes call for dipping the tortilla into sauce prior to filling and others call for covering the enchiladas with sauce after the tortillas have been filled and rolled. Either method will produce delicious results.

After filling the tortilla, roll to form a tube shape and place in baking pan, seam side down. Bake in a moderate oven (350 degrees) 20-30 minutes or in a microwave until heated. If making enchiladas ahead, cover with foil and refrigerate. If pouring enchilada sauce over all, do this just before baking so that the tortillas do not become soggy.

Five Minute Enchiladas

FLOUR TORTILLAS, medium size
1 cup CHEESE, grated
1 med. ONION, chopped
1 can (15 oz.) ENCHILADA SAUCE

Sprinkle cheese and onion in center of each tortilla. Roll tortillas and place, seam side down, on plate. Microwave on high for 1 - 1 1/2 minutes. Cover each with equal amounts of sauce. Microwave again for 30 seconds.

Allow 2-3 enchiladas per serving.

Enchiladas con Queso

12 CORN TORTILLAS
1/3 cup VEGETABLE OIL
2 cups LONGHORN or MEDIUM CHEDDAR
    CHEESE, grated
6 GREEN ONIONS, chopped
1 can (4 oz.) diced GREEN CHILES, drained
1 can (15 oz.) ENCHILADA SAUCE
1/2 head LETTUCE, shredded

Soften tortillas in heated oil as directed in Enchilada Basics (see p. 77). One by one, sprinkle cheese, onions and chiles down the center of each tortilla. Roll tightly and place, seam side down, in a large baking dish. Spoon enchilada sauce evenly over the tortillas. Bake for 10-15 minutes in a medium oven, uncovered, or until hot. Top with shredded lettuce.

Allow 2-3 enchiladas per serving.

Mexican Pizza

FLOUR TORTILLAS, any size
SALSA

Toppings of choice:
- **grated cheese**
- **diced chiles**
- **cooked and chopped meat**
- **diced onions**
- **tomatoes**

Spread a thin layer of salsa over flour tortilla. Add toppings. Place on cookie sheet and broil until edges of tortilla turn light brown.

Allow 1 small or one-half large tortilla per serving.

Enchiladas con Pollo

12 CORN TORTILLAS
3 cups cooked CHICKEN, chopped
1 can (7 oz.) diced GREEN CHILES, drained
1 Tbsp. dried CILANTRO
1/4 tsp. ground CUMIN
1/4 tsp. ALLSPICE
1 cup JACK CHEESE, grated
2 cups ENCHILADA SAUCE
2 cups LETTUCE, shredded

Soften tortillas in hot oil as directed in Enchilada Basics (see p. 77). In a large mixing bowl, combine chicken, chiles, cilantro, cumin, allspice and half of the cheese. Toss gently. Distribute equally among the tortillas. Roll the tortillas and place, seam side down, in a large baking dish. Pour 1 cup of the enchilada sauce over enchiladas and bake in a 400 degree oven for 10 minutes. Remove from oven, sprinkle with remaining cheese and bake 5 more minutes. Top with shredded lettuce and serve the remaining cup of sauce in a gravy boat for those wishing more sauce.

Allow 2-3 enchiladas per serving.

Spinach Enchiladas

12 CORN TORTILLAS
2 pkgs. (10 1/2 oz. each) frozen chopped SPINACH
1/4 tsp. ground NUTMEG
2 cups JACK CHEESE, grated
1/4 cup ONION, diced
1 tsp. crushed RED PEPPERS (from jar)
1 cup JACK CHEESE, grated
1 cup fresh CILANTRO, chopped

Soften corn tortillas in hot oil as described in Enchilada Basics (see p. 77). Cook spinach according to package directions and drain thoroughly. In a medium bowl, combine spinach, cheese, onion and red peppers. Fill tortillas evenly with spinach mixture and roll tightly. Place seam side down in a large baking dish. Place under broiler on bottom shelf until tortillas are piping hot. To serve, sprinkle with extra cheese and cilantro.

Allow 2 enchiladas per serving.

Haystack Enchiladas

Haystack enchiladas are left flat and stacked like a torte. They are also called New Mexican enchiladas. Occasionally these enchiladas are incorrectly called "Flat Enchiladas." A flat enchilada, also called a Sonoran enchilada in reference to its place of origin, is a small pancake, usually about half an inch thick, that is deep fried. A flat or Sonoran enchilada is made from masa dough.

12 CORN TORTILLAS
3 cups LONGHORN CHEESE, grated
1 cup ONION, diced
3 cups ENCHILADA SAUCE
1 cup GREEN OLIVES, sliced
3 cups LETTUCE, finely shredded

Fry tortillas in vegetable oil, one at a time, until slightly crispy, turning once with tongs. Do not fold. Drain between layers of paper towels. Place 4 tortillas on a baking sheet, sprinkle a small amount of cheese and onion and spoon a tablespoon of sauce on each stack. Repeat this layering until each stack has 3 tortillas, ending with cheese and onion on top. Bake in a 350-degree oven until cheese bubbles.

Serve with green olives and lettuce sprinkled over the stacks. Serve extra sauce if desired.

Serves 4.

Beef Enchiladas

12 CORN TORTILLAS
1 lb. GROUND BEEF
1 med. ONION, diced
1 can (4 oz.) sliced BLACK OLIVES
2 cups LONGHORN CHEDDAR CHEESE, grated
2 cans (15 oz. each) SALSA VERDE
1 pt. carton SOUR CREAM
1 can (4 oz.) diced GREEN CHILES, drained

Prepare tortillas as described in Enchilada Basics (see p. 77). Drain on paper towels and set aside. Sauté ground beef and onion until beef is cooked. Drain if necessary. Spoon about 2 tablespoons of meat mixture down the center of each tortilla, then an equal amount of olives, cheese and salsa, reserving half the salsa. Roll tortillas and place seam side down in baking pan. Bake at 350 degrees for 20 minutes. While enchiladas are baking, stir chiles into sour cream. Serve sour cream mixture and extra salsa at the table.

Allow 2-3 enchiladas per serving.

Note: 2 cups of shredded beef roast can be used in place of ground beef.

An Enchilada is a tortilla, usually corn, filled
with any combination and rolled
or stacked in layers.

Burrito Basics

Burritos are Mexican sandwiches that are made by filling a flour tortilla and rolling the tortilla, tube-like, so it can be eaten by hand like a sandwich. Burritos are sometimes called burros. Burritos that are deep fried or baked are called chimichangas. Usually the fillings for burritos are simpler than those used for chimichangas. Burritos are the perfect way to use up leftovers.

Beef & Bean Burritos

8 FLOUR TORTILLAS 10-12 inch size
1 lb. GROUND BEEF, cooked
1/4 cup ONIONS, chopped
1/2 cup REFRIED BEANS
1 cup LONGHORN CHEESE, grated

Heat each tortilla in a large ungreased frying pan. Place the beef, onions, beans and cheese in the center of the tortilla. Roll the tortilla and eat like a sandwich.

Serves 6-8.

Broccoli Burritos

1 pkg. (10 1/2 oz.) frozen chopped BROCCOLI
1 sm. ONION, diced
1 cup JACK CHEESE, grated
1 pkg. burrito size FLOUR TORTILLAS

Cook broccoli according to package directions. Drain well. In a bowl, combine broccoli, onion and cheese. Place equal amounts of the broccoli mixture in the center of each tortilla. Roll tortillas, tube-like and secure with a toothpick. Place seam side down on a baking dish and bake in a 375 degree oven until heated and the cheese is melted. (Remove toothpicks before serving.)

Makes 10-12 burritos.

Chimichanga Basics

Chimichangas have become popular in recent years. Not only are they easy to prepare but they offer an endless variety of one dish meals. A traditional chimichanga is made with a 10-12 inch flour tortilla wrapped around a filling and folded, envelope-style, then deep fried until crispy. When flour tortillas are deep fried, they become pastry-like; layered, delicate and crispy. Miniature versions, using 6 inch flour tortillas, make wonderful appetizers and snacks. Chimichangas can also be prepared by baking in a very hot oven, 450 degrees, until golden brown. This is a good alternative for those who prefer to avoid fried foods. Whether fried or baked, place the filled tortilla, seam side down, turning once with tongs while cooking in either a medium size skillet or on a baking sheet.

Chimichangas are usually served with salsa, chopped tomatoes and lettuce on the side. A chimichanga that is served "Enchilada Style" means that it is covered with enchilada sauce and cheese.

Chimichangas del Mar

12 (12-inch) FLOUR TORTILLAS
2 cups cooked SEAFOOD (shrimp, lobster, crabmeat
    or a combination)
2 cups JACK or other mild white CHEESE, shredded
1/2 cup GREEN ONIONS, sliced in 1/2-inch pieces

Combine seafood, shredded cheese and onions in a large mixing bowl. Divide the mixture equally among the 12 tortillas. Fold in sides of each tortilla and roll. Using your hands, dampen each rolled tortilla with cold water. Place on large baking sheet, seam side down, in a 500 degree oven. Bake until golden brown.

Allow 2-3 chimichangas per serving.

Chile Chimichangas

These chimichangas are delicious and different. They are a combination of chimichangas and chile rellenos and have a delicate flavor.

10 (10-12 inch) FLOUR TORTILLAS
2 cans (7 oz. each) whole GREEN CHILES
1 lb. JACK CHEESE
VEGETABLE OIL for frying

Wash chiles, removing seeds. Lay chiles out on paper towels and blot dry. Cut cheese in 2-3 inch "sticks" and wrap inside each chile. One by one, place cheese filled chiles in the center of the tortillas and fold the tortillas, envelope-style, around the filled chiles. Heat oil, about 1/2 inch, in a medium size frying pan. Place filled tortillas, seam side down, in hot oil and fry until golden brown. Turn only once to brown the other side. Drain on paper towels.

Allow 2 chimichangas per serving.

Bean Chimichangas

6 (10-12 inch) WHOLE WHEAT FLOUR TORTILLAS
1 can REFRIED BEANS
1 1/2 cups LONGHORN or CHEDDAR CHEESE, grated
1/2 cup ONIONS, diced
SALSA

Spoon beans down middle of tortillas, distributing them equally among the six tortillas. Sprinkle equal amounts of cheese and onion on beans. Fold sides of tortillas toward the center and roll up, envelope-style. Place on baking sheet and bake in a 450 degree oven for 15 minutes or until golden. Serve with salsa.

Makes 6 chimichangas. Allow 1-2 per serving.

Beef Chimichangas

1/4 cup VEGETABLE OIL
6 (10-12 inch) FLOUR TORTILLAS
1 lb. GROUND BEEF, cooked and drained, if necessary
1/2 cup ONION, diced
1 can (7 oz.) diced GREEN CHILES, drained
2 TOMATOES, diced
SALSA

Heat vegetable oil in a frying pan large enough to hold a rolled tortilla. In a medium bowl, combine the cooked ground beef, onion, chiles and tomatoes. Divide equally between the tortillas and roll each, envelope-style. Fry seam side down in vegetable oil until crispy. Drain on paper towels. Allow 1-2 chimichangas per serving. Serve with salsa.

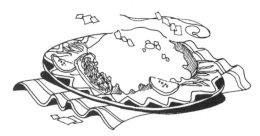

Salsa por Chimichangas

1/3 cup OIL (not olive oil)
1 med. ONION, minced
2 GARLIC CLOVES, minced
1 can (15 oz.) TOMATOES, chunk style, drained
1 Tbsp. CHILI POWDER
1 tsp. ground CUMIN
1 can (4 oz.) diced GREEN CHILES

Heat oil, sauté onions and garlic until onions become limp. Add remaining ingredients and simmer slowly 5 minutes.

Makes 3 cups.

Empanada Basics

Empanadas are little pies that are filled with meats or other fillings. In some areas they are a holiday tradition when filled with mincemeat. They are wonderful all year and so versatile that they stir the imagination.

Empanadas can be cooked by frying in 1 1/2 inches of vegetable oil in a deep frying pan until golden brown on both sides. If preferred, empanadas can be baked. To use the baking method, brush each empanada with melted butter and place on a baking sheet. Bake in a 375 degree oven for approximately 20 minutes or until golden brown. If making a dessert empanada, sprinkle 1/4 teaspoon of granulated sugar on the buttered pie before baking.

Easy Empanadas

Some filling suggestions include leftover roast beef or roasted chicken or canned pie filling.

1 pkg. tube CRESCENT ROLLS, found in the dairy case, usually in packages of 10
1 1/2 cups FILLING OF CHOICE.

Place 2 tablespoons filling in the center of each unrolled crescent. Roll up dough as directed on package and cook according to one of the methods described.

Allow 2 empanadas per serving.

Pollo con Frijoles Negro

(Chicken with Black Beans)

2 whole or 4 half cooked CHICKEN BREASTS
1 can (15 oz.) BLACK BEANS, drained
1/2 cup SALSA
1/2 cup WHITE WINE
1/2 tsp. ALLSPICE

Place chicken breasts on dinner plates. In small bowl, combine beans, salsa, wine and allspice. Top each chicken serving with bean mixture. Heat in microwave. Serve hot.

Serves 4 with half breast servings or 2 with whole breast servings.

Beans, called frijoles in Spanish, are a basic food of Mexico. There are many varieties available; fresh, dried and canned. Two of the most popular are pinto beans and black beans.

Pollo Español

4 boneless CHICKEN BREASTS
2 Tbsp. LIME JUICE
1 tsp. dried CILANTRO
1 tsp. CHILI POWDER
1 Tbsp. OLIVE OIL

Place chicken in large skillet. In small bowl, combine the remaining ingredients and pour over chicken. Cook covered, over medium high heat, for 30 minutes. Remove lid, turn chicken and continue cooking until chicken is done. Serve with pan drippings.

Serves 4.

Side Dishes

Zucchini Fritters

These can be made with any squash that is available. They are delicious served with salsa.

2 lbs. ZUCCHINI, grated
1 cup FLOUR
2 EGGS
2 Tbsp. ONION, grated
1 can (7 oz.) diced GREEN CHILES
VEGETABLE OIL

Combine zucchini, flour, eggs, onion and chiles and mix well. Drop by tablespoonful in heated vegetable oil until browned and crispy. Drain well on paper towels.

Makes 12 fritters. Allow 3-4 fritters per serving.

Chile Cheese Squash

1 lb. ZUCCHINI, SUMMER or YELLOW SQUASH
1/2 cup MAYONNAISE
1 can (4 oz.) diced GREEN CHILES, drained
1/2 cup LONGHORN CHEESE, grated
1/2 cup BREAD CRUMBS

Cook squash in boiling water until just tender. Drain well. Return to saucepan, stir in mayonnaise, chiles, cheese and bread crumbs. Serve hot.

Serves 6-8.

Vegetable Medley

2 Tbsp. OLIVE OIL
4 cups ZUCCHINI, chopped
4 TOMATOES, chopped
1/2 cup ONION, diced
1/2 tsp. dried CILANTRO

1/8 tsp. ground CUMIN
1 Tbsp. dried PARSLEY
   FLAKES
1/8 tsp. GARLIC SALT

Sauté zucchini in olive oil in a large frying pan for 5 minutes, stirring frequently. Add tomatoes, onion, cilantro, cumin, parsley flakes and garlic salt. Cook another 15 minutes over medium-high heat, stirring frequently.

Serves 6-8.

Baked Hominy

2 cans (15 oz. each) white HOMINY
1 can (7 oz.) diced GREEN CHILES
1 can (10 1/2 oz.) CHEDDAR CHEESE SOUP
1/8 tsp. PEPPER
1 tsp. dried CILANTRO (from jar)
1 cup SOUR CREAM
1 cup LONGHORN or MEDIUM CHEDDAR CHEESE, grated

Place hominy in colander and rinse well with cold running water. Allow to drain. Preheat oven to 375 degrees. In large bowl, combine drained hominy and all other ingredients except cheese. Place in baking dish and bake for 45 minutes. Remove from oven, sprinkle cheese on top and return to oven until cheese melts and is bubbly.

Serves 6.

Fried Corn

4 slices BACON
3 cups CORN, fresh or canned
2 tsp. SUGAR
1 cup MILK
1 Tbsp. FLOUR
SALT & PEPPER to taste

In a large skillet, fry bacon until crispy. Remove from pan and drain on paper towels. Drain all but one tablespoon of bacon fat from skillet. Add corn, sugar, bacon (crumbled) and salt and pepper to taste. Cook over medium heat until corn is lightly brown, stirring constantly. Combine milk and flour, pour slowly over corn mixture, stirring constantly until thickened.

Serves 4.

Pronto Tamale Casserole

4 green corn TAMALES, frozen, fresh or canned
1/2 lb. Mexican style VELVEETA® CHEESE, grated
1 can (7 oz.) diced GREEN CHILES, drained
4 EGGS
1/4 cup FLOUR
2 cups MILK

Cut tamales in bite-sized pieces and place in a lightly buttered, ovenproof baking dish. Top tamales with cheese and chiles. Beat eggs, add flour, beat until smooth and add milk. Pour over casserole and bake, uncovered, in a 375 degree oven for 1 to 1 1/4 hours or until done.

Serves 4.

Baked Chiles & Onions

6 lg. white (sweet) ONIONS, sliced
2 sm. or 1 lg. JALAPEÑO, peeled, seeded and sliced thin
2 Tbsp. BUTTER
3 Tbsp. FLOUR
1 cup MILK
3/4 cup ALMONDS, slivered

Separate onions into rings and boil gently in lightly salted water to cover until tender. Drain and set aside. Melt butter in a medium skillet, stir in flour and slowly add milk to make a cream sauce. Add jalapeños and almonds to sauce. Remove from heat. Place onions in a medium, lightly buttered casserole dish, pour sauce over all and bake in a 350 degree oven for 30-45 minutes or until casserole is set and lightly browned on top.

Serves 4.

Bean Pancakes

2 cans (15 oz.) REFRIED BEANS
FLOUR
1 cup CHEESE, grated
SOUR CREAM, if desired

Empty beans into a medium bowl. Slowly add enough flour to make the bean mixture hold together. Form into 3-inch patties and grill on a non-stick frying pan until browned and toasted on each side. Remove from pan, top with cheese and sour cream, if desired. Allow 2-3 cakes per serving.

Makes 12 cakes.

Frijoles Deluxe

4 Tbsp. OLIVE OIL
1 GARLIC CLOVE, crushed
1 med. ONION, diced
1 tsp. dried CILANTRO
2 cans (14 to 15 oz. each) whole PINTO BEANS, drained
SALSA

Sauté garlic, onions and cilantro in the olive oil until onions are limp but not browned. Stir in beans. Heat and serve with salsa, if desired.

Serves 4-6.

Chile Rice

2 1/2 cups cooked RICE
1 can (7 oz.) diced GREEN CHILES
2 cups SOUR CREAM
1 cup LONGHORN or CHEDDAR CHEESE, grated

Combine all ingredients in a large bowl. Pour into a well buttered baking dish. Bake in a 350 degree oven for 30 minutes or microwave on high for 5 minutes or until hot and bubbly.

Serves 4.

Mexican Rice

1 cup uncooked RICE
3 Tbsp. OLIVE OIL
1 med. ONION, diced
2 med. TOMATOES, chopped
1/4 tsp. GARLIC POWDER

1 Tbsp. diced GREEN CHILES
1 Tbsp. diced pickled JALAPEÑO
2 cups CHICKEN BROTH

Rinse and drain rice, set aside. Heat oil in a large skillet. Sauté onion until lightly browned. Add rice and sauté until golden. Add remaining ingredients, cover skillet tightly and simmer over very low heat for 30 minutes.

Serves 4.

Spanish Rice

6 slices BACON
2 med. ONIONS, diced
4 cups cooked RICE
1/4 tsp. ground ALLSPICE
1 jar (2 oz.) diced PIMENTOS, drained
1/2 cup BELL PEPPER, diced
1 can (15 oz.) TOMATOES, drained
1 cup LONGHORN or MEDIUM CHEDDAR CHEESE, grated
FLAVORED PEPPER, to taste

In medium skillet, cook bacon until crisp. Drain on paper towels and set aside. Add onion and cook until lightly browned. In large bowl, combine rice and remaining ingredients. Add bacon and onions and combine well. Place rice mixture in lightly buttered medium casserole and bake in 350 degree oven for 45 minutes.

Serves 6.

Lemon Rice

This is a wonderful dish served with fish or seafood.

2 cups WATER
1/4 cup LEMON JUICE
1/4 cup LIME JUICE
1 Tbsp. grated LEMON RIND
1 cup regular uncooked RICE

Combine water, lemon and lime juice and lemon rind in medium pan. Bring quickly to boil, reduce heat and add rice. Simmer gently, covered, for 30 minutes, until all the liquid is gone.

Serves 4.

Red Potatoes

2 lbs. POTATOES, cubed
2 Tbsp. crushed RED PEPPER, from jar
1 Tbsp. dried PARSLEY FLAKES
1 tsp. SALT
4 Tbsp. BUTTER

In a large saucepan, cook cubed potatoes. Drain potatoes thoroughly. Return to pan. Add remaining ingredients and toss gently to coat potatoes. Serve hot. Wonderful with beef. Use any leftovers chilled in a salad.

Serves 6.

Fried Potatoes

(Papas Fritos)

1/4 cup VEGETABLE OIL
1 med. ONION, diced
1 lb. POTATOES, diced
2 cans (7 oz. each) whole GREEN CHILES, cut into strips

Heat oil in large skillet over medium heat. Sauté onions until limp but not browned. Add potatoes and chiles, cover and cook over low heat until potatoes are tender. Remove cover, turn heat to medium-high and cook until potatoes and onion are lightly browned.

Serves 4.

Mexican Potatoes

4 BAKING POTATOES, sliced 1/4 inch thick
1 cup BUTTER, melted
1 Tbsp. MEXICAN SEASONING, from jar (found in spice and
seasoning center in the market)

Cover baking sheet with foil, dull side up to avoid burning. Arrange potatoes evenly on sheet. Mix butter and seasoning and spread evenly over potatoes. Bake in 375 degree oven for 30 minutes or until potatoes are cooked.

Serves 4-6.

Desserts

Sonoran Pumpkin Cookies

Pumpkin, a very rich source of Vitamin A, is grown widely in Mexico and is a great favorite for all kinds of cooking.

1/2 cup VEGETABLE OIL
1 cup BROWN SUGAR
1 EGG
1 cup PUMPKIN, mashed
1 3/4 cups FLOUR
1 cup BRAN FLAKES
1/2 cup WALNUTS, chopped
1/2 tsp. SALT
1 tsp. ground CINNAMON
1/2 tsp. ground CLOVES
1/2 tsp. ground NUTMEG
1 tsp. BAKING SODA
1/2 cup RAISINS

In a large bowl, mix oil, sugar, egg and pumpkin. Beat well. In a second large bowl, combine all the remaining ingredients. Combine the two mixtures, stirring until completely blended. Drop by the teaspoonful on a lightly greased baking sheet. Bake in a 375 degree oven for 15 minutes.

Makes about 4 dozen cookies.

Sopaipillas

Sopaipillas are little pillow-shaped puff breads that can be filled with honey, cinnamon and sugar or with jams and jellies. They are traditionally eaten as a dessert but can be enjoyed at any time.

2 cups FLOUR
1/2 tsp. SALT
2 tsp. BAKING POWDER
2 Tbsp. SUGAR
1 Tbsp. SHORTENING
3/4 cup MILK
VEGETABLE OIL

In a large bowl, combine flour, salt, baking powder and sugar. Cut in shortening and add milk, a little at a time, until the dough is just firm enough to roll. Cover bowl with a towel and let dough rise for one hour. Roll out dough on a lightly floured board and cut into 3-inch squares. Pour about 2 inches of oil into frying pan and heat to medium high. Drop a few pieces of dough at a time into hot oil. Cook until golden brown, turning once. Drain on paper towels.

Makes about 3 dozen.

Lime Sours

3/4 cup BUTTER or MARGARINE
1/2 cup SUGAR
1 1/2 cups FLOUR
2 EGGS
1/4 tsp. BAKING POWDER
1 cup BROWN SUGAR
1 cup PECANS, chopped
juice of three LIMES
2 tsp. LIME PEEL
1 Tbsp. BUTTER or MARGARINE
POWDERED SUGAR

In a medium bowl, mix the 3/4 cup of butter or margarine, sugar and flour. Press mixture into a lightly buttered 8 x 8 ovenproof baking pan. Bake at 325 degrees for 15 minutes. While this is baking, combine eggs, baking powder, sugar and pecans in a medium bowl. Pour over first mixture and bake again for 20 minutes. In a large bowl, stir together lime juice, lime peel, butter and enough powdered sugar to make a spreading consistency. Spread over hot mixture in pan. Cool completely, cut into squares.

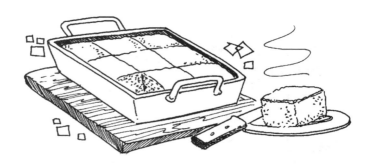

Special Oatmeal Cookies

2 1/2 cups FLOUR
1 tsp. BAKING SODA
1 1/2 tsp. SALT
1 tsp. ground CINNAMON
1/4 tsp. ground CLOVES
1/4 tsp. ground NUTMEG
2 cups ROLLED OATS (not instant)
1 cup WALNUTS, chopped
1 cup RAISINS
2/3 cup SHORTENING
1 cup SUGAR
2 EGGS
1 cup SOUR MILK

In a large bowl, combine flour, soda, salt, cinnamon, cloves and nutmeg. Add rolled oats, walnuts and raisins. Mix well. In another large bowl, cream together shortening, sugar, eggs and milk. Combine mixtures well. Drop by the teaspoonful on a lightly greased baking sheet. Bake in a 400 degree oven for 20 minutes.

Makes about 5 dozen cookies.

Caramel Corn

Corn is grown throughout Mexico and is used mainly for corn tortillas. However, there is no limit to the recipes that use corn in some way. Popcorn is also a favorite throughout the country.

6 qts. popped POPCORN
1/2 lb. (2 sticks) BUTTER or MARGARINE
1/2 cup light CORN SYRUP
2 cups BROWN SUGAR
1/2 tsp. BAKING SODA

In a medium saucepan, combine butter, syrup, brown sugar and baking soda. Boil gently for 5 minutes. Pour over popcorn and stir well. Place coated popcorn mixture in a large ovenproof baking dish and bake in a 250 degree oven for one hour, stirring every 15 minutes. Remove from oven, stir every 5 minutes until cooled.

Saltillo Corn Pudding

Saltillo is a charming town in east-central Mexico where this dessert was discovered.

4 cups hot MILK
1/2 cup CORNMEAL
1/2 cup MAPLE or OTHER SUGAR SYRUP
1/4 cup MOLASSES
2 EGGS
2 Tbsp. BUTTER or MARGARINE
1/2 cup BROWN SUGAR
1/3 tsp. ground CINNAMON
1 tsp. ground GINGER
1/2 cup cold MILK

In a medium saucepan, heat milk until very hot but not boiling or scorched (a microwave is not recommended for this recipe). Stir cornmeal into milk and simmer very gently, stirring occasionally, for 20 minutes. In a medium bowl, combine all of the remaining ingredients, except the cold milk. Add to the cornmeal mixture, stir well. Pour into a lightly buttered pie pan or 2 quart ovenproof baking dish. Without stirring, pour cold milk over the mixture. Bake in a 300 degree oven for 2 hours. Let stand for 45 minutes before serving.

Serves 6.

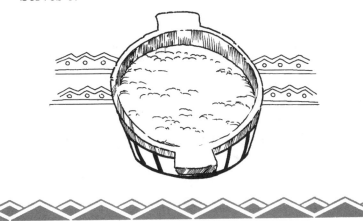

Flan

Flan is Mexico's most famous dessert. It has become a favorite everywhere. (It takes a while to make, but it's worth it!)

1 cup WHITE SUGAR
1 can SWEETENED CONDENSED MILK
1 1/2 cups HEAVY CREAM
1/2 tsp. ground CINNAMON
4 EGGS

Heat sugar in skillet over medium high heat. When sugar begins to melt, lower heat and stir until sugar is caramelized. Pour into one-quart baking dish, rotating to coat the sides. In medium bowl, combine milk, cream, cinnamon and eggs. Pour mixture over sugar. Place baking dish in pan of hot water so that water comes halfway up the sides of baking dish. Bake in 325 degree oven for 1 hour and 45 minutes or until knife inserted in center comes out clean.

Serves 6-8.

Strawberries Kahlua

3 cups fresh STRAWBERRIES, hulled
1 cup WHIPPING CREAM
1/4 cup KAHLUA®

Combine all ingredients and chill well. Serve in sherbet cups.

Serves 4.

Citrus Sours

Citrus grows in many areas of Mexico as a major commercial crop. These cookies can be made with any citrus or combination of citruses.

1 cup BUTTER, softened
1/2 cup LIGHT BROWN SUGAR
1/2 cup WHITE SUGAR
1 EGG
1/4 tsp. BAKING SODA
2 Tbsp. fresh LIME JUICE
1 Tbsp. grated LIME RIND
1 1/2 cups FLOUR
1/2 cup PECANS or WALNUTS, chopped fine

Cream together butter and both sugars. Add egg, beat well. Add remaining ingredients and blend until smooth. Chill 1 hour. Drop by the teaspoonful on ungreased cookie sheet. Bake in 375 degree oven for 8-10 minutes. Cookies should be slightly browned at the edges. Allow to cool at least 1 1/2 hours.

Makes about 3 dozen cookies.

Mexican Wedding Cakes

2 1/2 cups FLOUR
1/3 tsp. ground CINNAMON
1 cup BUTTER, softened
1 cup PECANS, chopped fine
1/2 cup POWDERED SUGAR
1 1/2 tsp. VANILLA EXTRACT
POWDERED SUGAR

In large bowl, combine flour and cinnamon. Add butter, pecans, powdered sugar and vanilla. Stir well. Using your hands, shape into 1-inch balls. Bake on ungreased baking sheet in 400 degree oven for 10-12 minutes. Roll in powdered sugar when removed from oven. When cool, roll in powdered sugar again.

Makes about 4 dozen cakes.

Unknown Fudge

3 cups SUGAR
1 1/2 cups WHIPPING CREAM
3 Tbsp. light CORN SYRUP
2 1/2 Tbsp. INSTANT COFFEE (a flavored variety, if desired)
2 Tbsp. BUTTER or MARGARINE
1 1/2 tsp. VANILLA EXTRACT
1 1/2 cups NUTS, chopped, if desired

Spray non-stick cooking spray or butter a large saucepan. Combine sugar, cream, corn syrup and coffee. Bring to a boil, stirring constantly. Cook until small amount dropped into glass of cold water forms a soft ball. Remove from heat, add butter, vanilla and nuts. Do not stir. Let mixture rest until it reaches room temperature, then beat until it begins to stiffen. Pour into well buttered 8 x 8 inch pan. Cool completely before cutting into squares.

NOTE: This is called unknown fudge because its origins have been long lost. Once flavored coffees became available, the author began to try different ones with delicious results. Amaretto is a great favorite. The recipe calls for vanilla extract. In Mexico vanilla extract, rather than artificial vanilla flavoring, is used in cooking. Vanilla extract is widely available in better stores.

Beverages

Classic Margarita

4 oz. TEQUILA
2 oz. TRIPLE SEC®
2 cups LEMON-LIME MIX
SALT
ICE
LEMON or LIME wedges

Combine the tequila, Triple Sec and lemon-lime mix in a cocktail shaker with ice. Shake well. Rub the cut lemon or lime around glass rim and dip into salt. Strain the margaritas into two glasses.

Serves 2.

Summer Margaritas

This delicious summer version of the Classic Margarita is served in a large glass with plenty of ice and a sprig of fresh mint.

1 cup each:
TEQUILA
TRIPLE SEC®
FRESH LIME JUICE

Blend in blender and pour equal amounts into 4 tall glasses. Fill glasses almost to the top with either LEMON-LIME SODA or GRAPEFRUIT SODA. Add ice cubes to each glass.

Serves 4.

Fruit Flavored Margarita

MARGARITA recipe
FRESH FRUIT, if available
   or FRUIT FLAVORED LIQUEUR

   Prepare Classic Margarita according to directions. Add fresh fruit of choice or liqueur to margarita. Blend together.

Tequila Daiquiri

1/2 cup TEQUILA
1 tsp. SUGAR
1/4 cup LIME JUICE

   Combine ingredients with ice and shake well. Pour into chilled glasses.

Tequila Sunrise

1 1/3 cups ORANGE JUICE
1/4 cup LIME JUICE
1/2 cup TEQUILA
2 1/2 Tbsp. GRENADINE
MINT SPRIGS for garnish

   Combine orange and lime juices with tequila. Pour into three ice filled glasses. Slowly add grenadine to each glass. Add a sprig of fresh mint to each glass.

   Serves 3.

Tequila Slush

1 1/2 cups TEQUILA
1 can (6 oz.) frozen LIMEADE
1 cup ORANGE JUICE
1 cup CRUSHED ICE (or 10-12 ICE CUBES)

Place in blender and blend on high until mixed and slushy.

Serves 4.

Mucho Mary

Days on the beaches of Mexico would not be complete without this great drink. It is equally delicious with or without tequila.

1 cup TOMATO JUICE, fresh or canned
1 cup CLUB SODA
ICE CUBES
slices of LIME
2 oz. TEQUILA, if desired

Pour tomato juice and club soda into tall glass over ice. Garnish with lime slices.

Mexican Martinis

1 cup very dry VERMOUTH
4 cups GIN or VODKA
12 ICE CUBES
pickled JALAPEÑOS

Place vermouth, gin or vodka and ice in cocktail shaker. Shake well to chill. Strain into martini glasses. Add jalapeno, on a toothpick, to each glass.

Makes 6 cocktails.

Tutti Frutti

1 can (6 oz.) frozen ORANGE JUICE
1 can (6 oz.) frozen LIMEADE
6 oz. TEQUILA, rum or bourbon
ICE CUBES, about 2 cups
4 whole STRAWBERRIES

Combine ingredients, except strawberries, in blender and liquefy. Add ice cubes, a few at a time, until all are liquefied. Pour into old fashioned glasses and top with whole strawberry.

Serves 4.

Sangria

Sangria is a sweet punch or cooler that, like the margarita, has endless varieties and flavors.

1 bottle light or rosé WINE
1/2 cup TEQUILA
1 cup ORANGE JUICE
1/4 cup SUGAR
2 LIMES, sliced very thin

Combine wine, tequila, orange juice and sugar. Mix well. Pour over ice cubes. Add lime slices to each glass. Dilute with orange or lemon-lime soda, if desired.

Serves 6.

Naco Special

2 cups TOMATO or V-8® JUICE
1 Tbsp. LIME JUICE
1 tsp. WORCESTERSHIRE SAUCE
1/2 cup TEQUILA

Combine all ingredients and shake well with ice.

Mexican Chocolate I

6 oz. DARK SWEET CHOCOLATE
1 tsp. ground CINNAMON
1/8 tsp. pure VANILLA EXTRACT
1/8 tsp. ALMOND EXTRACT
3 cups MILK

Melt chocolate in microwave. Stir in cinnamon, vanilla and extracts. Add to milk. Serve warm.

Serves 3.

Mexican Chocolate II

4 cups MILK
4 oz. SWEET CHOCOLATE
1/8 tsp. ground CINNAMON

Heat milk and chocolate together until chocolate is melted. Stir in cinnamon. Whip until frothy with hand mixer or in a blender. Serve warm.

Serves 4.

Cocoa Coffee

1 package HOT COCOA MIX, any flavor
1 cup hot COFFEE

Prepare hot cocoa mix according to package directions, substituting coffee for the hot water. Stir well to dissolve cocoa mix.

Mexican Ranch Coffee

10 cups COLD WATER
5 Tbsp. GROUND
**   COFFEE**
1 Tsp. SUGAR

WHIPPED CREAM, if desired
GROUND CINNAMON, or
**   CINNAMON STICK, per mug**
**   if desired**

Combine first three ingredients and bring to a gentle boil. Remove from heat and let grounds settle for 5 minutes. Pour through strainer into mugs, add whipped cream to which ground cinnamon has been added, if desired.

Makes 10 cups.

Summer Coffee

This is a great dessert coffee on a warm summer evening.

Follow the directions for Mexican Ranch Coffee, omitting the whipped cream. Place coffee in blender, add one pint vanilla or coffee ice cream. Liquefy in blender. Serve in mugs.

Café de Olla

Mexico is famous for its exceptional coffee. Coffee is a widely used addition to many recipes.

4 cups strongly brewed COFFEE
3 cups LIGHT CREAM

1/3 cup BRANDY
1/3 cup RUM
1/3 cup CREME DE CACAO

Simmer together in large pan, preferably earthenware. Do not allow to boil.

Serves 6.

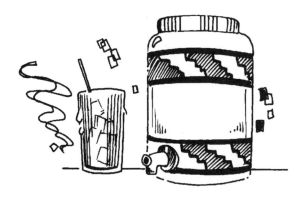

Sun Tea

Sun tea is a great favorite in Mexico. Sun tea is crystal clear and mellow in flavor. Don't be discouraged from brewing delicious tea if you haven't seen the sun recently. Follow the same directions and allow the tea to brew for several hours in the refrigerator.

2 qts. COLD WATER • 1/2 cup loose TEA or 6 TEA BAGS

Combine water and tea in a large jar. Cover and place in sun or in refrigerator for 6-8 hours. Strain tea, add lemon or lime slices, if desired.

Kahlua After Dinner

1 pt. VANILLA ICE CREAM, softened
1/2 cup KAHLUA®
1 cup black COFFEE
> Combine in blender and blend well. Serve in mugs.

> Serves 4.

Mexican Eggnog

1 qt. commercial EGGNOG
1 cup RUM or BRANDY
CINNAMON STICKS

Combine the eggnog and rum, or brandy, and chill. Serve with cinnamon sticks.

> Serves 5.

Mexican Coffee Pot Tea

This is a wonderful way to make iced tea.

2 tsp. per cup LOOSE TEA   **2 COFFEE FILTERS**
COLD WATER

In an electric coffee maker, place two filters. Add 2 teaspoons of loose tea per cup of water. Brew as for coffee. Serve over ice cubes, or hot, if desired.

Allow one cup per serving.

Mexican Hot Cocoa

1/4 cup COCOA
1/4 cup SUGAR
3/4 tsp. CINNAMON

1 qt. WHOLE MILK
1/3 cup HEAVY CREAM
1 tsp. VANILLA

Combine cocoa, sugar and cinnamon. Set aside. Heat 1 cup of milk until bubbly, stir in cocoa mixture, mix with wisk until smooth. Gradually stir in remaining milk so slow boiling continues. Remove from heat, stir in cream and vanilla. Mix well.

Makes 5 cups.

Not all of Mexico's favorite beverages contain spirits. Mexican coffees and chocolates are delicious and fresh fruit punches are widely available. Flavored teas are becoming popular everywhere and are wonderful served hot or cold.

Mexican Coffee

4 cups WATER
1/3 cup DARK BROWN SUGAR
1/2 cup INSTANT COFFEE
4 CINNAMON STICKS

Combine water and sugar, bring to a boil, stirring until sugar is dissolved. Reduce heat and stir in coffee, simmer two minutes. Pour into individual mugs, add a cinnamon stick to each mug. Stir coffee with stick.

Makes 4 cups.

Index

About the Author

Susan K. Bollin is a geologist and an author. She has written extensively in the fields of earth science and environmental science for both adults and children. In addition, she has written books for dog, cat and horse owners. Most recently, Ms. Bollin has written cookbooks about southwestern and Mexican foods. In addition to *Quick-n-Easy Mexican Recipes*, she is also the author of *Salsa Lovers Cook Book* and *Chip and Dip Lovers Cook Book*. She and her family live in Arizona.

Salsa Lovers Cook Book

More than 180 recipes for salsa, dips, salads, appetizers and more!
$9.95

Quick-n-Easy Mexican Recipes

Make your favorite Mexican dishes in record time! Excellent tacos, tostadas, enchiladas and more!
$9.95

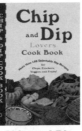

Chip and Dip Lovers Cook Book

Easy and colorful recipes from Southwestern salsas to quick appetizer dips!
$9.95

Tortilla Lovers' Cook Book

Celebrate the tortilla with more than 100 easy recipes for breakfast, lunch, dinner, appetizers and desserts, too!
$9.95

Chili Lovers Cook Book

Prize-winning recipes for chili, with or without beans. Plus a variety of taste-tempting foods made with flavorful chile peppers.
$9.95

Arizona Cook Book

A collection of authentic Arizona recipes. Including Indian, Mexican and Western foods.
$9.95

New Mexico Cook Book

This unique book explores the age-old recipes that are rich with the heritage of New Mexico.
$9.95

Easy RV Recipes

Easy recipes for the traveling cook. Over 200 recipes to make in your RV, camper or houseboat.
$9.95

Easy Recipes for Wild Game

More than 200 "wild" recipes for large and small game, wild fowl and fish.
$9.95

Apple Lovers Cook Book

What's more American than eating apple pie? Try these 150 favorite recipes for appetizers, main and side dishes, muffins, pies, salads, beverages and preserves.
$9.95

Pumpkin Lovers Cook Book

More than 175 recipes for soups, breads, muffins, pies, cakes, cheesecakes, cookies and even ice cream! Carving tips, trivia and more.
$9.95

Mexican Family Favorites Recipes

250 authentic, home-style recipes for tacos, tamales, menudo, enchiladas, burros, salsas, frijoles, chile rellenos, carne seca, guacamole, and more!
$9.95

QTY	TITLE	PRICE	TOTAL
	Burrito Lovers' Cook Book	9.95	
	Chili Lovers' Cook Book	9.95	
	Chip & Dip Lovers' Cook Book	9.95	
	Citrus Lovers' Cook Book	9.95	
	Easy BBQ Recipes	9.95	
	Easy BBQ Sauces	9.95	
	Grand Canyon Cook Book	9.95	
	Low Fat Mexican Recipes	9.95	
	New Mexico Cook Book	9.95	
	Mexican Family Favorites Cook Book	9.95	
	Quick-n-Easy Mexican Recipes	9.95	
	Salsa Lovers' Cook Book	9.95	
	Sedona Cook Book	9.95	
	Tequila Cook Book	9.95	
	Texas Cook Book	9.95	
	Tortilla Lovers' Cook Book	9.95	
	Veggie Lovers' Cook Book	9.95	
	Western Breakfast	9.95	

US Shipping & Handling Add	1-3 Books: 5.00	
[for non-domestic ship rates, please call]	4-9 Books: 7.00	
	9+ Books: 7.00 + 0.25 per book	
	AZ residents add 8.3% sales tax	

(US funds only) Total:

Please make checks payable to:
Golden West Publishers
4113 N. Longview,
Phoenix, AZ 85014

☐ Check or money order enclosed
☐ MC ☐ VISA ☐ Discover ☐ American Express Verification Code:_____

Card Number:_____ Exp._____
Signature: _____
Name_____Phone: _____
Address _____
City_____State_____ZIP _____
Email _____

Prices are subject to change.

Recipe:_____

From:_____

Ingredients:

_____   _____

_____   _____

_____   _____

_____   _____

_____   _____

Directions:_____

_____

_____

_____

_____

Recipe:_____

From:_____

Ingredients:

_____   _____

_____   _____

_____   _____

_____   _____

_____   _____

Directions:_____

_____

_____

_____

_____

Recipe:_____

From:_____

Ingredients:

_____   _____

_____   _____

_____   _____

_____   _____

_____   _____

Directions:_____

_____

_____

_____

_____

Recipe:_____

From:_____

Ingredients:

_____   _____

_____   _____

_____   _____

_____   _____

_____   _____

Directions:_____

_____

_____

_____

_____